Close Reading Companion

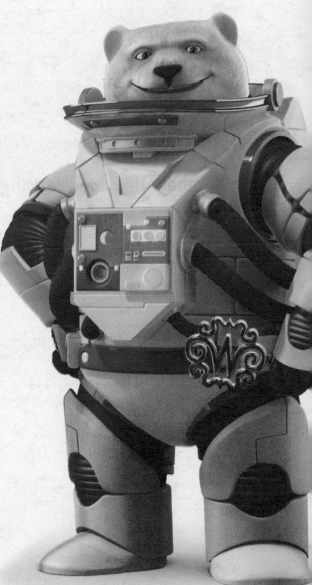

Mc
Graw
Hill
Education

Cover and Title Page: Nathan Love

www.mheonline.com/readingwonders

Send all inquiries to:
McGraw-Hill Education
Two Penn Plaza
New York, New York 10121

ISBN: 978-0-02-130649-7
MHID: 0-02-130649-4

Printed in the United States of America.

7 8 9 10 LMN 22 21 20 19

D

CHANGES

UNIT 1

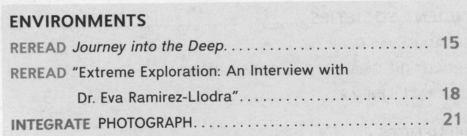

Excursions Across Time

CONTRIBUTIONS

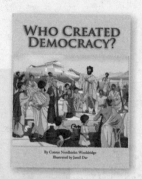

DEMOCRACY

ANCIENT SOCIETIES

INFLUENCES

PAST AND PRESENT

DEA/G. DAGLI ORTI/De Agostini Picture Library/Getty Images; Erich Lessing/Art Resource - NY; Frans Lemmens/Photodisc/Getty Images; Emanuele Taroni/Photodisc/Getty Images; Steve Taylor/Photographer's Choice/Getty Images

ACCOMPLISHMENTS

COMMON GROUND

TRANSFORMATIONS

INSPIRATION

MILESTONES

TIME FOR KIDS

Challenges

CHANGING ENVIRONMENTS

OVERCOMING CHALLENGES

STANDING TALL

SHARED EXPERIENCES

TAKING RESPONSIBILITY

Discoveries

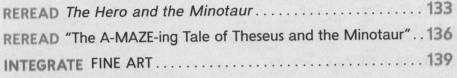

UNIT 6

Taking ACTION

Little Blog on the Prairie

Literature Anthology:
pages 10–23

? How does the author use dialogue to help you understand how the
characters feel?

COLLABORATE

Talk About It Reread the dialogue on page 15. Talk about how Gen's family
deals with life at the camp.

Cite Text Evidence What words and phrases tell you how the characters feel?
Cite and explain text evidence.

Dialogue	What Happens	How Characters Feel
"You want it raw?" "I'm hungry."	Gavin asks to eat grits raw because he is so hungry.	Gavin feels hungry and impatient

Write The author uses dialogue to _____

_____

CLOSE READING

Tip of the Week

When I **reread**, I think about
how the author uses dialogue
to help me understand how
the characters feel.

Teresa

Steve Debenport/E+/Getty Images

How does the author create tension between Nora and Gen?

Talk About It Reread pages 16–17. Talk with a partner about what you notice about how Nora and Gen interact.

Cite Text Evidence What clues help you know how Nora feels about Gen? Find evidence and explain how it creates tension.

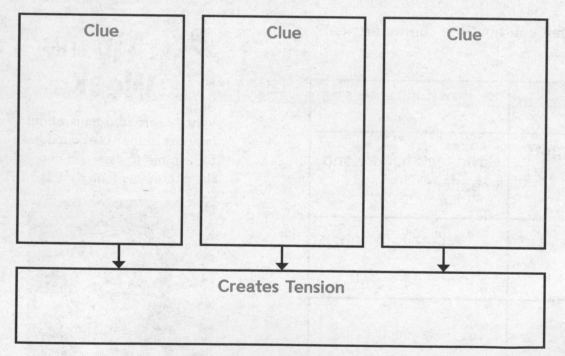

Clue	Clue	Clue

Creates Tension

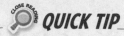 **QUICK TIP**

I can use these sentence frames when we talk about Gen's reaction to Nora.

Gen's description suggests she feels . . .

The author uses Nora to . . .

Write The author creates tension between Nora and Gen by _____

_____

_____

_____

? How does the author use Gen's text messages to help you understand how she is dealing with her new experience?

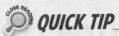

COLLABORATE

Talk About It Reread the text messages on page 20 and the first paragraph of page 21. Talk with a partner about why the text messages are important to the story.

Cite Text Evidence What words and phrases in Gen's text messages tell you about how she feels? Record evidence in the chart.

Text Evidence	How It Helps

Write The author uses Gen's text messages to show _____

_____

_____

Your Turn

How does the author help you understand how new experiences can change the way we think? Use these sentence frames to organize your text evidence.

The author uses dialogue . . .

Gen's point of view . . .

Having this perspective allows readers to . . .

Go Digital!
Write your response online.

The Writing on the Wall

[1]   The small town of Allen Crossing, Indiana, has been the place I've called home for all 14 years of my life. That's where I spend hours just looking. Looking at how the wind makes the wild flowers of a meadow weave and sway to create a magical moving carpet of color. Looking at the way insects dart and dash among plants and blossoms in displays of frantic activity.

[2]   The beauty and drama of nature have always been what drives me to create art. I used to think that all true artists get inspiration from nature. Then I went to New York City and something happened that really made me rethink that idea.

[3]   I applied to an art college in New York that was offering two-week courses to middle school students with portfolios that showed they were serious about art. To be honest, I applied mostly because I like the idea of putting my portfolio up against the work of other young artists. I wanted to see if I could get in.

Underline words and phrases in paragraph 1 that shows how the narrator feels about Allen Crossing.

Reread paragraph 2. Circle how you know what the narrator thinks about inspiration.

COLLABORATE

Talk with a partner about where the narrator has always found his inspiration. How do you know that his opinion will change later in the story?

Make a mark in the margin beside the sentences that signal change. Write them here:

_____

_____

_____

1   "It's a legal graffiti exhibit space." Myles said, "like a big gallery for street art." He explained that he and LeShawn and Pete had been selected to paint there in a contest their school had held before summer recess. They showed me sketches of what they planned to paint, and then I turned my gaze to the factory again. What I saw was art not unlike what I had been making. The big difference was, along with images from nature, the artists also drew images from city life. There was a subway train crammed with people rushing off to work and there were tall, shiny buildings stretching up into the sky. In every sketch, there was an energy that reminded me of that first subway ride, only it was a creative energy, not a panicky energy.

2   What I learned that summer in New York was indispensable to me, for now I know that inspiration is different for everyone. What drives one person crazy can be the thing that drives another to create. I may not look at the city the way Myles, LeShawn, and Pete do, but they may not see nature the way I do. I respect the way the city's energy inspires them.

Reread paragraph 1. Underline clues that show the narrator is changing his point of view about art.

Place a star beside the sentence that expresses his new perspective.

COLLABORATE

Reread paragraph 2. Circle phrases that show how the narrator feels about inspiration. Talk about the two lessons he has learned. Number the sentences in the margin beside the sentences. Write them here:

1. _____

_____

2. _____

_____

? **How does the author show a change in the narrator from the beginning to the end of the selection?**

COLLABORATE

Talk About It Reread the excerpts on pages 4–5. With a partner, discuss how the narrator feels about inspiration.

Cite Text Evidence Compare and contrast the narrator's feelings from the beginning to the end of the selection. Write text evidence in the chart.

Beginning	End

Write The author shows how the narrator changes by _____

_____

_____

_____

QUICK TIP

When I reread, I can use how the author uses point of view to teach me about how characters change.

? How is the sculptor in the photograph using art to share a perspective in the same way that the characters do in *Little Blog on the Prairie* and "The Writing on the Wall"?

QUICK TIP

I can find clues in the photograph that help me compare the sculptor to the characters I read about this week.

COLLABORATE

Talk About It Talk about the photograph and caption. Discuss how the girl is using art to express a new perspective.

Cite Text Evidence How does creating art show others how you feel? Circle clues in the photograph and caption that indicate how art can be a medium for sharing feelings and perspectives.

Write The sculptor and characters I read about this week use their art

_____

_____

_____

This middle school student is using a water-based clay to create a sculpture. The assignment was to think of someone she admires and create a piece of art that represents how she feels.

The Mostly True Adventures of Homer P. Figg

Literature Anthology:
pages 30–45

? How does the author use dialogue to help you understand Homer's relationship with his brother?

COLLABORATE

Talk About It Reread the last three paragraphs of page 33. Talk with a partner about what Homer says to Harold.

Cite Text Evidence What does Homer say that helps you understand how he feels about Harold? Write text evidence in the chart.

Text Evidence	Homer's Character

Write The dialogue helps me understand that Homer feels _____

_____

CLOSE READING

Tip of the Week

When I **reread**, I think about what the characters say to make inferences about who they are.

Miles

Bellurget Jean Louis/Stockbyte/Getty Images

How does the author create suspense?

Talk About It Reread the left column on page 35. Talk with a partner about what Harold tells Homer to do. Discuss how Homer responds.

Cite Text Evidence What clues create an uneasy feeling that something bad could happen? Write your response in the chart.

Clues	Inference

Write The author creates suspense by _____

_____

_____

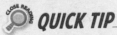 *QUICK TIP*

I can use these sentence frames when we talk about how the author makes me feel.

I read that Harold told Homer to . . .

That makes me feel . . .

? **How do the illustrations help you understand Homer's character and motives?**

Talk About It Examine the illustrations on pages 40 and 41. Talk with a partner about how they help you understand Homer's actions.

Cite Text Evidence What clues in the illustrations help you understand what Homer is doing? Fill in the web.

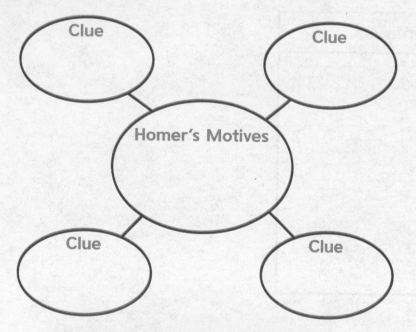

Clue

Clue

Homer's Motives

Clue

Clue

Write I learned from the illustrations that Homer _____

_____

_____

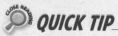

QUICK TIP

I can analyze illustrations to help me understand the character's motives.

Your Turn

How does the author help you understand how Homer changes from the beginning of the story to the end? Use these sentence frames to organize your ideas.

At the beginning, Homer tells his brother . . .

Rodman Philbrick uses dialogue to . . .

The dialogue between Homer and his brother shows . . .

Go Digital!
Write your response online.

Enough

I finish, glance at the clock.

There are fifteen minutes left.

Should I turn in my test? No.

Because I can hear Ernesto already. Ernesto
and his friends.

The snide laughter. The smirks. Adversity in all
its forms.

Hey Brainiac! Finished already?

*Too bad the Olympics don't have an event for
geeks!*

The bell finally rings. We turn in our papers.

Do I bolt out the door to avoid a cruel jeer?

Stay glued to my seat admitting my fear?

How much longer do I have to deal with this?

**Reread and use the prompts to take notes in
the text.**

Reread the excerpt. Circle words and phrases that
describe Jonas.

Underline words and phrases that describe Ernesto.

COLLABORATE

Talk with a partner about how you know what Jonas
is thinking. Make a mark in the margin beside the
text evidence that supports your discussion. Write the
evidence here:

_____

_____

_____

_____

My mind is in a whirl.

I feel bad about what I did.

But then I say to myself, what does it matter?

Sean did not see me.

And I also feel as if a large burden has been lifted off of me.

But why do I need to tear someone down to feel worthwhile?

The next morning is warm and sunny. A hint of spring.

I arrive at school early and sit outside.

The first students arrive.

And then I see Sean. I shout out his name and smile.

We shake hands.

An alliance is formed.

Then there is a loud noise behind us.

Hey Sean! It's Ernesto. A voice laced with disdain.

Hey Ernesto! I shout back. **Enough!**

Reread the excerpt. Circle words and phrases that help you know how Jonas is feeling.

Make marks in the margin beside the text evidence that shows what Jonas is thinking. Write his thoughts here:

_____

_____

_____

_____

COLLABORATE

Talk with a partner about how the mood of the poem changes. Underline the sentence that shows that change.

? **How does the poet use Jonas's thoughts to help you understand how he changes?**

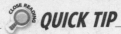

Talk About It Reread the excerpts on pages 11 and 12. Talk with a partner about how Jonas talks to himself at the beginning and end of the poem.

Cite Text Evidence What words and phrases show how he feels at the end of the poem? Write text evidence in the chart.

Jonas Thinks	How He Feels

Write The poet helps me understand how Jonas changes by _____

_____

_____

_____

? How does the poet show how the narrator changes in the poem similar to the way the authors show how the characters change in *The Mostly True Adventures of Homer P. Figg* and "Enough"?

COLLABORATE

Talk About It Read the poem. Talk with a partner about what the narrator does in the first two stanzas. Then discuss what happens at the end of the poem.

Cite Text Evidence Circle the words and phrases the poet uses to tell what the narrator does. Then underline two things the narrator discovers. Think about how Homer and Jonas change in the stories you read this week.

Write The poet and the authors show how characters change

by _____

_____

_____

QUICK TIP

The poet uses phrases to show how the narrator changes. This will help me compare text to poetry.

The Arrow and the Song

I shot an arrow into the air,
It fell to earth, I knew not where;
For, so swiftly it flew, the sight
Could not follow it in its flight.

I breathed a song into the air,
It fell to earth, I knew not where;
For who has sight so keen and strong,
That it can follow the flight of song?

Long, long afterward, in an oak
I found the arrow, still unbroke;
And the song, from beginning to end,
I found again in the heart of a friend.

— Henry Wadsworth Longfellow

Exactostock/SuperStock

Journey into the Deep

? Why does the author want you to visualize what a massive jellyfish looks like?

Talk About It Reread the first paragraph on page 51. Talk with a partner about how the author uses descriptive language to describe the jellyfish.

Cite Text Evidence Why is the author's description of the jellyfish important to the selection? Write your text evidence in the chart.

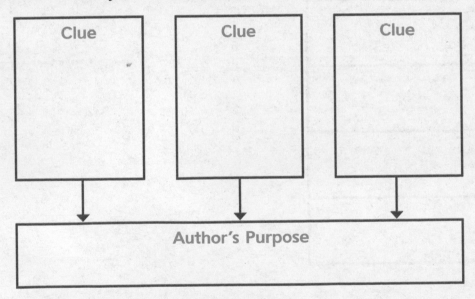

Clue	Clue	Clue

Author's Purpose

Write The author wants me to picture the massive jellyfish because _____

_____

Literature Anthology: pages 50–65

Tip of the Week

When I **reread**, I can analyze how the author uses words and phrases. I look for text evidence to answer questions.

Tyler

Arthur Tilley/Stockbyte/Getty Images

? **How does the author use text features to help you understand what it's like under the ocean?**

COLLABORATE

Talk About It Look at the text features on pages 54–55. Talk with a partner about how each text feature helps you know more about the ocean.

Cite Text Evidence What new information did you learn from the text features? Write it here.

Text Features	Evidence

Write The author's use of text features helps me _____

_____

_____

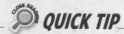
QUICK TIP

I can use these sentence frames when we talk about text features.

The photographs . . .

In the sidebar, I read that . . .

? **Why does the author use figurative language to describe life around the vents?**

COLLABORATE

Talk About It Reread page 63. Talk with a partner about what you visualize as you read how the author describes the vents.

Cite Text Evidence What words and phrases describe what life is like around the vents? Write evidence in the web.

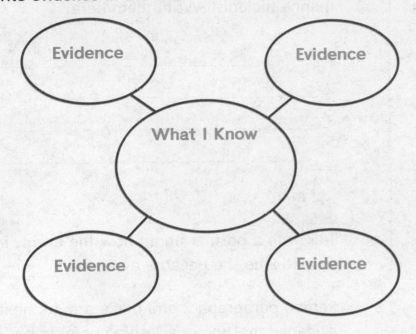

Evidence

Evidence

What I Know

Evidence

Evidence

Write The author uses figurative language to _____

_____

_____

QUICK TIP
I can visualize what the author wants me to know about life around the vents.

Your Turn

How does the way the author organizes information in this selection help you understand how she feels about ocean environments? Use these sentence frames to organize your ideas.

Rebecca Johnson uses text features to . . .

She also writes about . . .

This helps me understand that she thinks . . .

Go Digital!
Write your response online.

Extreme Exploration: An Interview with Dr. Eva Ramirez-Llodra

1   Imagine being eleven-years-old and having your parents announce one day that your family is about to take off on an eight-year adventure, sailing around the world. That's exactly what happened to Dr. Eva Ramirez-Llodra. She literally grew up at sea, and then when she turned nineteen, Eva returned to her native Barcelona, Spain to study biology. She couldn't have imagined then that the love for the sea she developed during that incredible trip would lead her to become a marine biologist.

2   In 1999 Dr. Ramirez-Llodra was chosen to become one of five coordinators for the Census of Marine Life project. Eva worked on this global effort with more than 2,500 other scientists. They explored deep-sea ecosystems all over the world for over ten years. The project's goal was to create a record of the biodiversity, or the different kinds of life that can be found in the world's oceans.

Reread and use the prompts to take notes in the text.

Reread paragraph 1. Circle how the author helps you imagine what happened to Dr. Eva Ramirez-Llodra when she was young.

Then underline the events that led to her career as a marine biologist. Write them here.

1. _____

2. _____

3. _____

   _____

COLLABORATE

Talk with a partner about how the events in Eva's life shaped who she became as an adult.

Reread paragraph 2 and make a mark next to the text evidence that shows a turning point in her career.

1   **Q:** Are there many creatures living in this unusual habitat?

Dr. Ramirez-Llodra: There are scientists who work on identifying different species. They analyze the different organisms and create a scientific classification so that types of creatures that are similar are grouped together. Scientists believe there may be over a million kinds of deep-sea life forms!

2   **Q:** How have these organisms adapted to life in this unique environment?

Dr. Ramirez-Llodra: These organisms don't suffer from the changing pressure underwater. That's because they don't have air inside their bodies. They have no difficulty moving in complete darkness. Some even use sound or light that they generate themselves to communicate with others of the same species. These special sounds and lights also distract predators, and attract prey. Many deep-sea species also have a reduced body density similar to the density of seawater. As a result, they neither sink to the sea floor nor float to the surface.

Reread question 1 and Dr. Ramirez-Llodra's answer. Underline how she answers the question. Then circle words and phrases that describe what scientists do.

COLLABORATE

Reread question 2 and Dr. Ramirez-Llodra's response. Number three ways she says that organisms have adapted to life in the unique underwater environment.

Talk with a partner about how the photograph helps you understand more about life under the ocean. Use text evidence and clues from the photograph to explain.

_____

_____

_____

_____

? How does the author help you understand how Dr. Eva Ramirez-Llodra feels about her life as a marine biologist?

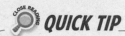
COLLABORATE

Talk About It Reread the excerpts on pages 18–19. Talk with a partner about how Dr. Ramirez-Llodra responds to the interview questions.

Cite Text Evidence What words and phrases help you see how Dr. Ramirez-Llodra feels? Use this chart to record text evidence.

Text Evidence	How She Feels

Write I know how Dr. Ramirez-Llodra feels about being a marine biologist

because _____

_____

QUICK TIP

When I reread, I use text evidence to support the inferences I make.

? How does the way the photographer helps you understand the polar bear's environment similar to how the authors of *Journey into the Deep* and "Extreme Exploration" help you visualize the ocean?

Talk About It Look at the photograph and read the caption. Talk with a partner about what you see and how the photographer uses her craft to help you understand how polar bears live.

Cite Text Evidence What clues in the photograph help you understand the polar bear's environment? Circle them. Then think about the photographer's craft. Underline parts of the photograph that show what she wants you to know.

Write I can understand what the photographer and authors want me to know because _____

_____

_____

_____

_____

_____

QUICK TIP

I see details in the photograph. This will help me compare it to the selections I read this week.

This polar bear walks on the ice near the open water in Alaska. He searches for seals to feed his family.

Into the Volcano: A Volcano Researcher at Work

Literature Anthology: pages 72–85

? How does the author present information to help you understand more about volcanoes?

COLLABORATE

Talk About It Look at pages 74–75. Talk with a partner about the different features of this selection and how they help you better understand volcanoes.

Cite Text Evidence How does the author help you understand the topic better? Use the chart below to show three ways she does this and how it helps you.

Tip of the Week

When I **reread**, I can analyze text features to help me understand more about a topic. Then I cite text evidence to answer questions.

How Volcanoes Form	Volcano Types	Diagrams

Abby

Write The author helps me understand more about volcanoes by _____

_____

_____

Glow Images

Why is "A Walk on the Wild Side" a good heading for this section?

COLLABORATE

Talk About It Reread page 79. Talk with a partner about how the author describes the lava tubes.

Cite Text Evidence What details help you visualize the danger of being so close to a lava tube? Write text evidence here.

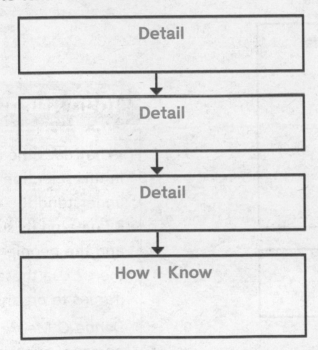

```
┌─────────────────────────┐
│         Detail          │
└─────────────────────────┘
            │
            ▼
┌─────────────────────────┐
│         Detail          │
└─────────────────────────┘
            │
            ▼
┌─────────────────────────┐
│         Detail          │
└─────────────────────────┘
            │
            ▼
┌─────────────────────────┐
│       How I Know        │
└─────────────────────────┘
```

Write "A Walk on the Wild Side" is a good heading for this section because ____

_____

_____

CLOSE READING
QUICK TIP

When I reread, I can analyze the author's word choice and how it helps me visualize information.

How do the author's real life experiences and descriptive language broaden your understanding of volcanoes?

COLLABORATE

Talk About It Reread the first three paragraphs on page 81. Talk with a partner about how the author makes reading about volcanoes exciting.

Cite Text Evidence How does the author's descriptive language help you visualize what she experienced? Record text evidence in the chart.

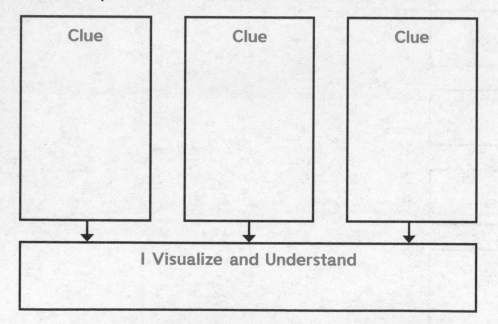

Clue	Clue	Clue

↓ ↓ ↓

I Visualize and Understand

Write The author helps me understand more about volcanoes by _____

_____

_____

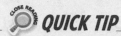
QUICK TIP

I can use these sentence frames when we talk about how the author describes her experience.

The author tells about her experience using . . .

These descriptions help me visualize . . .

Your Turn

What does the author do in this selection to help you understand the effects of Kilauea on its surroundings and the people who live there? Use these sentence frames to organize your ideas.

Donna O'Meara shares her personal experience . . .
She uses text features to . . .
This helps me understand that Kilauea . . .

Go Digital!
Write your response online.

Donna O'Meara: The Volcano Lady

1   After a blistering hot day, a cold storm suddenly whipped around the top of Mt. Stromboli, a volcano on an island off the coast of Sicily. The temperature quickly dropped over 60 degrees. Donna O'Meara and her husband, Steve, didn't dare try to climb down the steep slopes in the dark. They were stuck on a narrow ledge just 200 feet above a fiery, smoking pit. They huddled together, shivering nonstop in the cold air. Thundering blasts from the volcano and falling rocks the size of basketballs kept them awake and fearful. When the sun came up, Donna felt cinder burns on her face. There were sharp pieces of rock tangled in her hair.

2   Frightening experiences on top of a volcano are not unusual for Donna O'Meara. For over 25 years, she has worked with Steve to photograph and study volcanoes all over the world. They hope their documentation will someday be a written and visual record of information that helps scientists to better predict volcanic eruptions.

Reread and use the prompts to take notes in the text.

Circle words and phrases in paragraph 1 that the author uses to help you visualize what Donna experienced at the top of Mt. Stromboli.

Now reread paragraph 2 and underline the sentence that transitions from what she experienced to what she does. Write it here:

_____

_____

COLLABORATE

Talk with a partner about why the author chose to include such a vivid description of what Donna experienced.

Make marks in the margin next to the text evidence you used to support your discussion.

1   From their home, Donna and Steve run Volcano Watch International. (VWI) The O'Mearas' organization is dedicated to understanding how Earth's active volcanoes work. VWI uses photos and video to educate people about the dangers of volcanoes. Their mission is to travel to active volcanoes and document the eruptions.

2   The first volcano Donna studied was Kilauea, which is a shield volcano. Mt. Stromboli is a stratovolcano. A stratovolcano has the common cone shape people usually picture when they think of a volcano. It is formed from explosive eruptions that build layers of ash, lava, and cinders at the top of the mountain.

3   Donna says the experience of being stranded on Mt. Stromboli for one freezing night was the scariest experience of her life. Since the sides of this volcano are steep, it was impossible for the O'Mearas to travel down the slopes until the sun rose in the morning. So they were trapped on the ledge in the freezing cold with scalding rocks flying around them.

Reread paragraph 1. Underline Volcano Watch International's mission. Circle clues in the paragraph that describe what they do.

Place a star beside the sentence in paragraph 2 that helps you understand more about Mt. Stromboli.

COLLABORATE

Reread paragraph 3. Talk about why knowing the shape of a stratovolcano adds to your understanding of Donna's scary night on top of Mt. Stromboli.

Draw a box around one more clue that describes a stratovolcano.

Write it here:

_____

_____

_____

? How does the author show that Donna believes she has the best job on Earth?

COLLABORATE

Talk About It Reread the excerpts on pages 25 and 26. Talk with a partner about clues that help you figure out why the O'Mearas love what they do.

Cite Text Evidence What words and phrases does the author use to show that the O'Mearas love their job? Write text evidence below.

Clues	
	Donna and Steve O'Meara love their job.

Write I know Donna O'Meara loves her job because _____

_____

_____

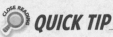 QUICK TIP

When I reread, I look for text evidence that helps me understand the author's point of view.

? How is the way the artist uses color and technique to paint the ocean similar to the way Donna O'Meara uses words and phrases to describe volcanoes in the selections you read this week?

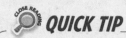

QUICK TIP

I can compare how an artist and an author use their craft to help me understand about Earth's natural forces.

COLLABORATE

Talk About It With a partner, talk about what you see in the painting. Talk about how the painting makes you feel.

Cite Text Evidence How does the feeling you get from looking at this painting compare to Donna's description of being stuck on top of Mt. Stromboli? Circle three clues in the painting that help you make that comparison.

Write Like O'Meara's description of volcanoes, Thomas

Chambers _____

_____

_____

_____

_____

Courtesy National Gallery of Art, Washington

American artist Thomas Chambers painted *Storm-Tossed Frigate* in the mid-nineteenth century. An oil painting on canvas, it is now owned by the National Gallery of Art in Washington, D.C.

The Economic Roller Coaster

Literature Anthology, pages 92–95

? How does the author help you understand the economy in a way that is relevant to you?

Talk About It Read the first two paragraphs on page 93. Talk about why the author uses real life examples to help you understand the topic.

Cite Text Evidence How does the author make the information relevant to you?

Text Evidence	How Is This Relevant?

CLOSE READING Tip of the Week

When I **reread**, I think about why the author includes certain information. I think about how that information connects to my life.

Victor

Write The author's real-life examples help me understand that the economy ___

_____

_____

Blend Images/Getty Images

? How does the author use text features to help you understand supply and demand?

COLLABORATE

Talk About It Look at the text features on pages 94–95. Talk with a partner about new information you learned and why the author includes them.

Cite Text Evidence How does each text feature help you understand supply and demand? Write the name of each text feature at the top of each column and how it helped below.

Write Text features help me understand supply and demand by _____

_____

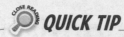
Your Turn

How does the sidebar help you understand a different point of view about the free-market economy in America? Use these sentence frames to organize your ideas.

The author of the feature believes . . .

I read that . . .

This helps me understand . . .

Go Digital!
Write your response online.

Our Federal Reserve at Work

1   Likewise, lower interest rates provide reasons for people to borrow more and save less. A low interest rate is likely to cause businesses to invest more and expand. It will also encourage people to make more purchases. In this way, interest rates affect how much economic activity takes place in an economy.

2   I believe that when the economy slows down the Federal Reserve must take action. It should lower interest rates and keep money moving through the economic system. I also believe the Fed should raise interest rates if people start borrowing too much.

3   The flow chart below helps explain this sound monetary position.

Reread and use the prompts to take notes in the text.

Reread paragraphs 1 and 2. Underline clues that help you understand the author's opinion about what the Federal Reserve should do. Then go back and circle evidence that supports the author's point of view.

Reread paragraph 3 and look at the diagram. Draw a box around a clue the author uses to persuade you to feel the same way she does.

COLLABORATE

Talk with a partner about how the text evidence and diagram work together to inform you about the economy and the author's opinion.

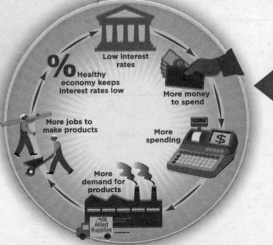

% Healthy economy keeps interest rates low

Low interest rates

More money to spend

More spending

More demand for products

More jobs to make products

Allied Supplies

The **Ripple** Effect
When the cost of borrowing money is at the right level, the entire economy runs smoothly.

How does the author persuade you to agree with her opinions about the Federal Reserve?

Talk About It Reread the excerpt on page 31. Discuss with a partner how the author states her opinions.

Cite Text Evidence What does the author say to persuade you to agree with her? Write text evidence in the chart.

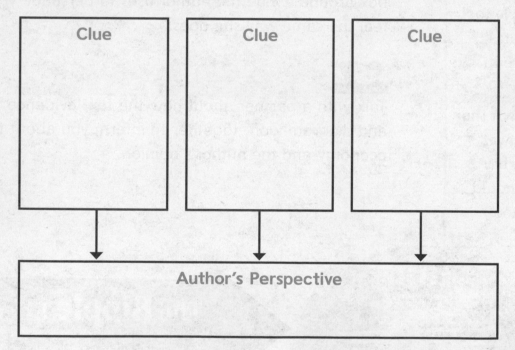

Clue	Clue	Clue

Author's Perspective

Write The author persuades me to agree with her opinions by _____

_____

_____

QUICK TIP

When I reread persuasive texts, I look for text evidence that supports the author's point of view.

Integrate

? How does the marketplace in the painting contribute to your understanding of the free market discussed in "The Economic Roller Coaster" and "Our Federal Reserve at Work"?

Talk About It Look at the painting and read the caption. Talk with a partner about how supply and demand discussed in "The Economic Roller Coaster" could impact the vendors in the painting.

Cite Text Evidence Circle examples in the painting of a free market economy. In the caption, underline text evidence that supports your discussion.

Write The painting deepens my understanding of the free market by _____

_____

_____

_____

_____

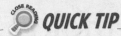

QUICK TIP

I can use details in this painting to help me understand the free market. I can compare it to the selections I read this week.

Flemish painter Pieter Angellis created this oil on copper painting of Covent Garden around 1726. Covent Garden is located in London's West End and has housed a fruit and vegetable market off and on since the 1600s.

The Technology of Mesopotamia

? What is the author's purpose for using the transitional word *however*?

Literature Anthology, pages 98–111

Talk About It Reread the last paragraph on page 101. Talk about what the author is comparing and how reading the word *however* makes you feel.

Cite Text Evidence What does the transitional word *however* help you understand about project planning? Use evidence from the text to complete this chart.

What I Read	What I Understand

Write The author uses the word *however* to _____

_____

Tip of the Week
CLOSE READING

When I **reread**, I can think about how the author uses transitional words. I look for text evidence to answer questions.

Isabel

Photomondo/Photodisc/Getty Images

? How do you know what the author's opinion is of the Mesopotamians' contribution to mail?

COLLABORATE

Talk About It Reread the section "Clay Envelopes" on page 106. Talk with a partner about how the Mesopotamians developed mail.

Cite Text Evidence What words and phrases tell how the author feels about the Mesopotamians' contribution? Write text evidence in the chart.

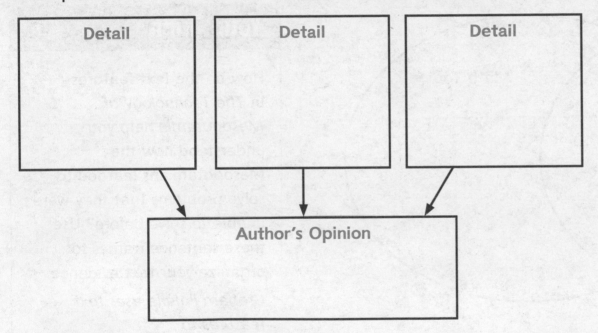

| Detail | Detail | Detail |

Author's Opinion

Write I know how the author feels about Mesopotamia's contribution to mail because he _____

_____

_____

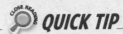

QUICK TIP

I can use these sentence frames when we talk about early mail delivery.

The author says that the Mesopotamians . . .

This helps me understand that he feels . . .

? How do the photograph and caption help you understand how the Mesopotamians influenced the number system we use today?

COLLABORATE

Talk About It Read the last two paragraphs on pages 108–109. Use the photograph and caption to talk about Mesopotamian math problems.

Cite Text Evidence Use the text, photograph and caption to compare Mesopotamian mathematics with mathematics today.

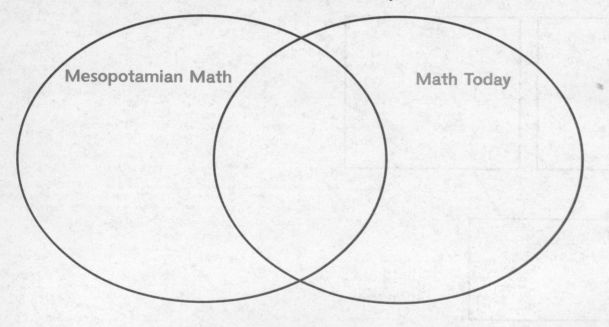

Mesopotamian Math   Math Today

Write The text features help me understand how _____

_____

_____

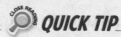

QUICK TIP

I can analyze photographs and captions to help me understand the text.

Your Turn

How do the text features in *The Technology of Mesopotamia* help you understand how the Mesopotamians learned to solve problems that they were unable to solve before? Use these sentence frames to organize your text evidence.

Graham Faiella uses text features to . . .

From the text features, I learned . . .

This is important because . . .

Go Digital!
Write your response online.

Gilgamesh Lost and Found

A Stunning Discovery

1   A dozen clay tablets tell what may be the first fictional story ever written on Earth. Yet the story was nearly lost forever. In 1853, archaeologists in Iraq discovered fragments of tablets covered with cuneiform writing. They turned out to be the remains of a vast Assyrian library that had been buried for more than two thousand years. But the cuneiform writing they contained was a mystery.

2   Then an amateur researcher named George Smith started studying the tablets. He taught himself all about cuneiform to record names, dates, and farming information. But then he found an artifact that was different from the rest. It told a story, the epic saga of King Gilgamesh. Epics are long narrative poems about the adventures and deeds of traditional or historical heroes or heroines.

Reread and use the prompts to take notes in the text.

Reread paragraph 1 and its heading. Circle the clues that help you understand how valuable the clay tablets are to history. Make a mark in the margin beside one clue that shows how the author feels about the discovery. Write it here:

_____

_____

COLLABORATE

Reread paragraph 2 with a partner. Talk about how the author transitions between the discovery of the tablets and George Smith's discovery of the artifact. Draw a box around the transition word.

Then underline how the author helps you know what an epic is.

The Epic of Gilgamesh

[1]   The epic begins in the Mesopotamian city of Uruk, where King Gilgamesh is a strong, brave, and handsome ruler. But he is also a selfish tyrant who mistreats his subjects and abuses his power. No one will challenge him, so the gods decide to send Enkidu to befriend Gilgamesh and hopefully bring peace.

[2]   In this excerpt, Enkidu and Gilgamesh meet for the first time.

[3]   Gilgamesh and Enkidu's friendship grows stronger as they travel and share many adventures. Returning at last to Uruk, Gilgamesh becomes a fair and compassionate king.

Gilgamesh and Enkidu

Put a star next to King Gilgamesh's good qualities. Circle the author's transition word that alerts you that Gilgamesh is not all good.

Underline why the gods decide to send Enkidu. Write it here:

_____

_____

COLLABORATE

Reread paragraph 3. Talk with a partner about how he describes how Gilgamesh changes from the beginning of the epic. Mark in the margin how Gilgamesh has changed.

Look at the illustration. Circle clues that help you understand how those changes happened.

? How does the author show the importance of George Smith's discovery?

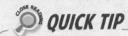 **QUICK TIP**

When I reread, I use how the author presents information to understand the text better.

COLLABORATE

Talk About It Use your notes and look back at both excerpts on pages 38–39. Talk about the importance of the discovery of the artifact.

Cite Text Evidence How does the way the author present information help you see how important Smith's discovery was? Write text evidence here:

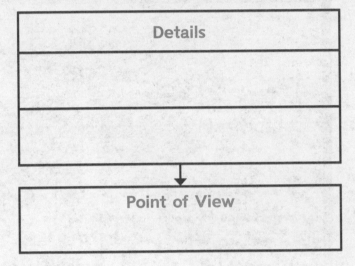

Details

↓

Point of View

Write I know how important George Smith's discovery was because the author _____

_____

? How does this sketch by Leonardo da Vinci compare to the artifacts discovered in both *The Technology of Mesopotamia* and "Gilgamesh Lost and Found?"

Talk About It With a partner, discuss what you see in Leonardo da Vinci's sketch. Read the caption and talk about why this sketch is important.

Cite Text Evidence Look at the sketch and reread the caption. Circle clues that help you see a connection between what Leonardo da Vinci envisioned and modern day helicopters. In the margin, make notes about how this sketch compares to the artifacts found in this week's selections.

Write The discovery of Leonardo da Vinci's sketch compares with discoveries from ancient civilizations because _____

_____

_____

_____

_____

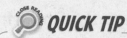

QUICK TIP

I see a connection between this sketch and modern day helicopters. This helps me compare text to art.

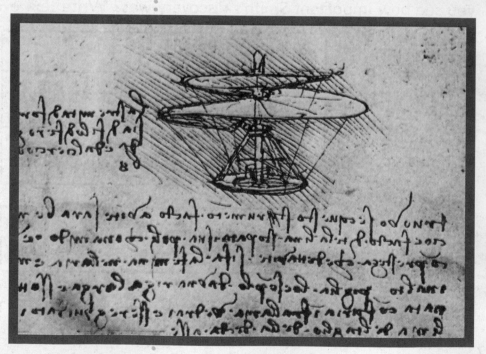

Claudio Divizia/Hemera/360/Getty Images Plus/Getty Images

Renaissance artist Leonardo da Vinci was also known as a scientist and inventor. This sketch of a helicopter was drawn in 1493, before mechanical engines were even invented.

Who Created Democracy?

? How does the author's description of the rich and the poor people in Athens help you understand how democracy was born?

Literature Anthology, pages 116–125

Talk About It Reread the first four paragraphs on page 118. Talk with a partner about the differences between the rich and the poor people in Athens.

Cite Text Evidence What words and phrases does the author use to compare the people of Athens? Record evidence in the chart and tell why it is important.

The Rich	The Poor	Why It's Important

Write The author's description of both rich and poor people helps me

understand how democracy was born by _____

_____

_____

Tip of the Week

CLOSE READING

When I **reread**, I think about how the authors use words and phrases. I look for text evidence to answer questions.

Kevin

Johnny Greig/E-plus/Getty Images

? **How does the author's use of idioms help you visualize the conflicts in Athens and the American colonies?**

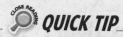

QUICK TIP

I can use these sentence frames when we talk about how the author uses figurative language

The author uses idioms to . . .
They create a mood that . . .

COLLABORATE

Talk About It Reread paragraphs 2–6 on page 120. Talk with a partner about the conflicts in ancient Athens and the American colonies.

Cite Text Evidence What idioms does the author use? Write them and explain them. Tell how they all help you visualize conflict.

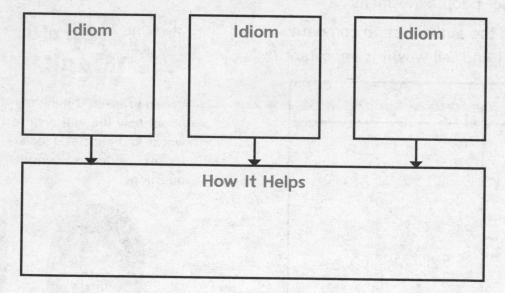

Idiom	Idiom	Idiom

↓ ↓ ↓

How It Helps

Write The author's use of idioms helps me to _____

_____

_____

_____

_____

Why does the author use transitional phrases?

COLLABORATE

Talk About It Reread page 124. Talk with a partner about how transitional phrases help you understand the events at the Constitutional Convention.

Cite Text Evidence What transitional phrases does the author use and how do they help you? Write text evidence here.

Transitional Phrases	Author's Purpose

Write The author uses transitional phrases to _____

_____

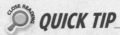 **QUICK TIP**

When I reread, I can focus on the how the author uses transitional phrases to help me understand the text.

Your Turn

Think about how Connie Nordhielm Wooldridge organizes information in this selection. How do her choices help you understand the development of democracy? Use these sentence starters to organize your ideas.

Connie Nordhielm Wooldridge compares and contrasts . . .

She also uses transitional phrases to . . .

She wants me to understand that . . .

Go Digital!
Write your response online.

How Ideas Become Laws

Democracy in Action

[1]   National laws apply to everyone in the United States, while state and local laws are for people who live in a particular state or city. Almost anyone can suggest a law.

[2]   Steve and his dad contacted Marta Ortiz, who was a member of the state assembly. Along with representatives in the state senate, assembly members make laws. After speaking with Steve, Ms. Ortiz agree that bicycle helmets were an important safety issue, so she said she would propose and sponsor a bill, or a plan for a law.

An Idea Becomes a Law

[3]   During a committee hearing with assembly members, Steve and Ms. Ortiz explained why they felt the law was necessary.   The committee rewrote the bill to include only people younger than 18 years of age, and then it passed it on to the assembly.   The assembly and the senate approved it, and   the governor signed it!

Reread and use the prompts to take notes in the text.

Reread paragraph 1. Circle what the author says about who can suggest laws.

Write it here:

_____

COLLABORATE

Reread paragraphs 2 and 3. Talk with a partner about the steps Steve and his dad take to try to get his idea to become a law.

In the margin, number the steps it took for Steve's idea to become a law.

A Law Takes Shape

Ms. Ortiz displayed the following chart to show Steve the process a bill takes to become a law in their state.

Step 1: The bill goes to a clerk, who reads the bill to the state assembly.

Step 2: The bill goes to a committee. If the committee approves the bill, it goes to the full state assembly.

Step 3: Representatives debate the bill then vote on it. If it passes in the assembly, it goes to the state senate.

Step 4: A state senate committee votes on the bill. If it passes, the full senate debates the bill then votes on it. If it is approved, it goes to the governor.

Step 5: The governor can sign the bill into law, do nothing so that it automatically becomes law after 5 to 14 days, or veto it. A veto means the law is rejected. Most state assemblies and senates can override a veto by a two-thirds majority vote.

Reread the chart. Circle the reason why Ms. Ortiz showed this chart to Steve.

COLLABORATE

Reread steps 1–5. Talk with a partner about who has a say in whether or not a bill becomes a law. Underline the text evidence.

Why is "A Law Takes Shape" a good title for this chart? Use text evidence and write your answer here:

_____

_____

_____

_____

_____

_____

? How does the sidebar help you understand the process Steve and his father went through to have an idea become law?

Talk About It Reread the excerpt on page 45. Talk about what you learn from the information in the sidebar.

Cite Text Evidence How do the steps in "A Law Takes Shape" connect with the steps Steve and his dad took? Write them in this chart.

"Democracy in Action"	A Law Takes Shape

Write The author uses a sidebar so I can see that _____

_____

_____

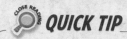
When I reread, I can use sidebars to understand more about the information presented in the selection.

? How is Tennyson's point of view of freedom similar to the authors' views of democracy in *Who Created Democracy* and "How Ideas Become Laws"?

COLLABORATE

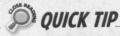

The poet uses imagery. This will help me compare it with the selections I read this week.

Talk About It Read the poem. Talk with a partner about what Tennyson compares freedom with. Discuss how the poet feels about freedom.

Cite Text Evidence Reread the poem. Circle words and phrases that describe what freedom does. Underline phrases that tell what freedom stands for. Think about how the authors feel about freedom in the selections you read this week.

Write Tennyson's description of freedom is like the authors'

descriptions of democracy because _____

_____

_____

Adeet Deshmukh/McGraw-Hill Education

Of Old Sat Freedom on the Heights

Of old sat Freedom on the heights,
  The thunders breaking at her feet:
Above her shook the starry lights:
  She heard the torrents meet. . . .

Grave mother of majestic works,
  From her isle-altar gazing down,
Who, God-like, grasps the triple forks,
  And, King-like, wears the crown:

Her open eyes desire the truth.
  The wisdom of a thousand years
Is in them. May perpetual youth
  Keep dry their light from tears;

That her fair form may stand and shine,
  Make bright our days and light our
  dreams,.

Turning to scorn with lips divine
  The falsehood of extremes!

— Alfred Lord Tennyson

Roman Diary

? How do the illustrations and captions help you understand more about Iliona and Apollo's new lives?

Talk About It Look at the illustrations on pages 132–133 and read the captions. Talk with a partner about how they add to what you read in Iliona's diary.

Cite Text Evidence What new information do you learn from the illustrations and captions? Compare it to what you read in the diary entry.

Iliona's Diary	Illustrations and Captions

Write The illustrations and captions help me understand that _____

_____

_____

*Literature Anthology,
pages 130–145*

Tip of the Week

CLOSE READING

When I **reread**, I can use illustrations and captions to help me understand the characters. I look for text evidence to answer questions.

Paige

Nikolay Titov/iStock/Getty Images

How does the author use figurative language to help you visualize what Etruscan Street was like?

COLLABORATE

Talk About It Reread the Day IV entry on page 134. Talk with a partner about how the author describes Etruscan Street.

Cite Text Evidence How does the description of Etruscan Street help you visualize what Iliona is experiencing? Write details in the web.

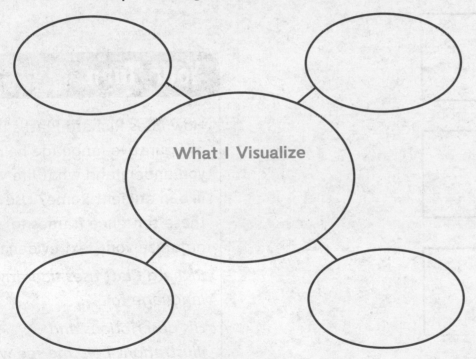

What I Visualize

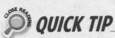
QUICK TIP

I can use these sentence frames when we talk about how the author describes Etruscan Street.

The author uses words like . . .

This helps me visualize . . .

Write The author's use of figurative language helps me visualize _____

_____

_____

? How does the author help you understand why Iliona saves Lydia from the fire?

Talk About It Reread the sixth paragraph on page 143. Talk about how the women respond to the fire and how it makes Iliona feel.

Cite Text Evidence What events led to Iliona's decision to save Lydia? Write text evidence in the chart.

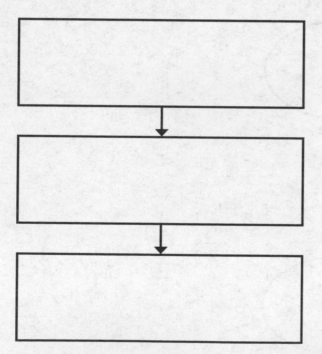

Write The author helps me understand why Iliona saves Lydia by _____

_____

_____

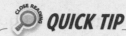
Your Turn

How does Richard Platt's use of figurative language help you understand what life was like in ancient Rome? Use these sentence frames to organize your text evidence.

Richard Platt uses figurative language to . . .

His descriptions and illustrations help me see why Iliona . . .

This is important because . . .

Go Digital!
Write your response online.

The Genius of Roman Aqueducts

[1]   Did you know that many children in ancient Rome did the same thing? In fact, they played many of the same games you do, jumping rope or playing catch, and when they were thirsty they came inside for a drink or went to any number of public drinking fountains around the city.

[2]   Most children in Rome knew how water was transported to their city. But did you ever wonder where the water you drink comes from? Or how it got to your faucet?

[3]   The fact is, if you do not have a well in your own backyard, the water you use at home may come from a long distance away. However, it doesn't travel by truck or train. Water is transported to you via a complex system of connected pipes and tunnels. These pipes and tunnels channel water from reservoirs and transport it to you. We call the system that carries water an aqueduct. In Latin, this word means "a conductor of water."

Reread and use the prompts to take notes in the text.

Reread paragraph 1. Circle the ways children in ancient Rome are like children today. Write them here:

Children in ancient Rome	Children Today
_____	_____
_____	_____
_____	_____

COLLABORATE

Talk with a partner about how the author invites you to keep reading. Reread paragraph 2 and make a mark in the margin beside how she does that.

Then reread paragraph 3. Underline how the author helps you understand what an aqueduct is.

1   The city of Rome was not different. It also grew up alongside a river, the Tiber, one of the longest rivers in Italy. But as Rome grew and became the capital of a large empire, it needed more water than the Tiber could provide. So how did the ancient Romans obtain and transport this water?

Aqueducts in Rome

2   Romans didn't invent the idea of aqueducts. They had been used in Mesopotamia to supply water to crops some distance from the Tigris and Euphrates. However, the aqueducts the Romans built were far more complex than anything that had come before them. Long, long before engines had been invented that could pump water, the ancient Romans figured out how to use natural forces to do the same thing. They used the water pressure created by gravity to move water hundreds of miles. It would travel from mountaintop lakes, down the sides of mountains, across valleys and into cities and towns.

In paragraph 1, circle the problem that occurred as Rome grew. How does the author transition into the next section? Underline the text evidence.

COLLABORATE

Reread paragraph 2 and look at the map. How does the author help you understand how the ancient Romans moved water? Make a mark in the margins where the author shows this. Write it here:

_____

_____

Circle clues in the map that show how water is transported into the city.

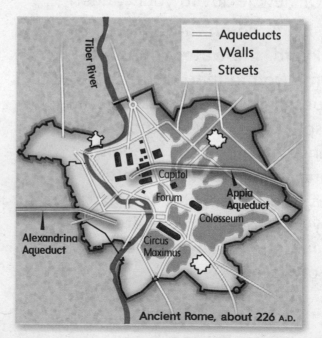

Legend:
- ═══ Aqueducts
- ▬ Walls
- ═══ Streets

Tiber River

Capitol
Forum
Appia Aqueduct
Colosseum
Alexandrina Aqueduct
Circus Maximus

Ancient Rome, about 226 A.D.

? **Why is "The Genius of Roman Aqueducts" a good title for this selection?**

 **QUICK TIP**

When I reread, I use text evidence to answer questions.

COLLABORATE

Talk About It Reread the excerpt on page 52. Talk with a partner about how the Romans built the aqueducts.

Cite Text Evidence What clues help you see how the Roman aqueducts were "genius." Record text evidence in the chart.

Text Evidence	Why It's Important

Write "The Genius of Roman Aqueducts" is a good title because _____

_____

_____

? How does this cave painting, Iliona's diary in *Roman Diary* and the aqueducts in "The Genius of Roman Aqueducts" help you understand what life was like in ancient cultures?

Talk About It Talk with a partner about what you see in the photograph of the cave painting. Focus on what is happening and what you might learn about the people who painted it.

Cite Text Evidence Look at the painting and read the caption. Circle clues that tell you something about how the people who created it lived.

Write The cave painting and selections I read this week help me understand about ancient cultures

by _____

_____

_____

_____

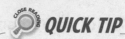

QUICK TIP

I can use the cave painting to learn something about the people who made it. This will help me compare art to text.

CAROLUS/age fotostock

This cave painting of a buffalo was found in France. People from all over come to see it.

A Single Shard

Literature Anthology, pages 152–167

? How does the author's use of a flashback help you understand more of Crane-man and Tree-ear's story?

Talk About It Reread the last two paragraphs on page 156 and all of page 157. Talk about how Tree-ear and Crane-man came to live together.

Cite Text Evidence What do you learn about Tree-Ear from this passage? Complete the chart with evidence from the text.

Text Evidence	Inference

Tip of the Week

When I **reread**, I can use literary devices to help me understand more about the characters and their motives.

Nicolás

Write The flashback helps me understand _____

_____

_____

_____

? **How does the author use sensory language to help you understand the culture of Ch'ulp'o?**

COLLABORATE

Talk About It Reread pages 160–161. Describe to a partner what you visualize about Ch'ulp'o's culture as you read the description of Min working.

Cite Text Evidence What words and phrases does the author use to paint a picture of the culture of Ch'ulp'o. Use the web below to record evidence.

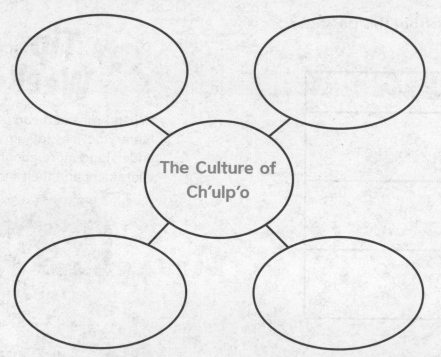

The Culture of Ch'ulp'o

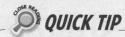 **QUICK TIP**

I can use these sentence frames when we talk about how the author uses sensory language.

The author describes how Min works using . . .

This helps me visualize . . .

Write To help me understand the culture of Ch'ulp'o, the author _____

_____

_____

? How does the way the author ends the story show how both Tree-ear and the town will change?

COLLABORATE

Talk About It Reread pages 166–167. Talk about what happens between Tree-ear and Min.

Cite Text Evidence How does the author show the plot events that lead to Tree-ear's new opportunity? Write them here.

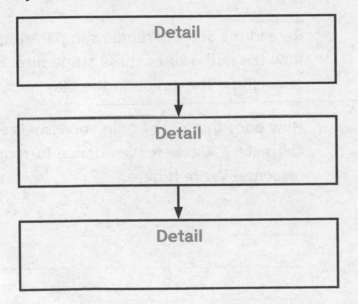

Detail

↓

Detail

↓

Detail

Write The author shows how Tree-ear and the town will change by _____

_____

_____

_____

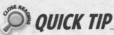
QUICK TIP
When I reread, I think about the way the author develops the plot and how each event leads to the next.

Your Turn

Think about Tree-ear's character and the culture of Ch'ulp'o. What parallels does Linda Sue Park draw between the development of a culture and the development of the main character? Use these sentence frames to organize your text evidence.

Linda Sue Park describes Tree-ear and Ch'ulp'o by . . .

She uses sensory language to . . .

This helps me understand how . . .

Go Digital!
Write your response online.

A Scholar in the Family

1   The history of China is filled with the struggles of leaders who tried to unite the people of this enormous country. Since the Sui Dynasty (581–618), it had been possible to become a government official by passing a series of written exams. It was only during the Song Dynasty (960–1279), however, that the examination system came to be considered the ladder to success.

2   Beginning around 1000, for the first time, Chinese commoners were permitted to have jobs within the government. These jobs were called civil service jobs. In order to qualify for a civil service job, men had to take a very grueling civil service exam.

3   **Narrator** *(Stands alone in front of curtain)*: Permit me to introduce you to Cheng. *(Cheng walks onto stage and bows.)* Cheng is a young scholar. He has studied very hard in order to take the civil service exam. He is far from home, taking this very difficult test right now.

Reread and use the prompts to take notes in the text.

Read paragraphs 1 and 2. Underline three facts about the development of the Chinese government.

Make a mark in the margin beside the sentence that foreshadows something a character in the play will do.

COLLABORATE

Reread the stage directions in paragraph 3. Talk about how the author uses these stage directions to help you understand the action in the play.

How does the author help you visualize Cheng's character? Circle text evidence to support your response. Write it here.

_____

_____

_____

1 **Grandfather:** Years ago, only men born to noble families could take the civil service examination. Commoners could not move up in the world. Today, any scholar may try his luck. Now, government jobs will come to those who have proven skill, and not because they were born into a noble house.

2 **Mother:** Only one scholar in 100 passes the test! But Cheng has worked so hard. His eyes would grow so tired, learning how to print thousands of Chinese characters. And he has spent years studying the teachings of Confucius, the great educator.

3 **Mei:** I know. "I helped him study by doing his chores sometimes, remember?" (*She smiles brightly.*)

4 **Grandfather:** Yes, and I was very proud of you. You were a great help to your brother. In my day if the earth trembled and our homes collapsed or if the great river overflowed, swollen with too much rain, and swept our fields away we peasants lost everything. We had no other work we could do – no way to earn money and rebuild our lives.

Read section 1. Underline the sentence that shows what taking the civil service examination means to commoners. Write it here:

_____

_____

Read the rest of the excerpt. Talk with a partner about how the family feels about Cheng taking the test. Circle evidence in the dialogue to support your discussion.

Julie Wu

? How does the author help you understand how important the test is to Cheng's family and future?

COLLABORATE

Talk About It Reread the excerpts on pages 58–59. With a partner, talk about how you know the civil service examination is important.

Cite Text Evidence What words and phrases does the author use to show how important the test is? Write text evidence in the chart.

Introduction	Family's Dialogue

Write The author helps me understand how important the test is by _____

_____

_____

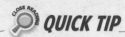

? How is the train track in this illustration similar to the clay in *A Single Shard* and the exam in "A Scholar in the Family"?

COLLABORATE

Talk About It Look at the illustration and read the caption. Talk with a partner about what is happening and how you know it depicts an important event.

Cite Text Evidence Circle clues in the painting and caption that show this is an important historical event. Draw a line down the center of the photograph. Then underline the two things that meet. Talk about the significance of transportation to the development of American culture.

Write This photograph, the clay, and the exam help us understand

_____

_____

_____

_____

Architect of the Capitol

CLOSE READING

QUICK TIP

I see an important event depicted in this illustration. This will help me compare text to art.

GOLDEN SPIKE

This illustration is based on a historic photograph taken on May 10, 1869. It shows where the last spike was driven in Promontory Point, Utah. This is the place where the Union Pacific and Central Pacific railroads met to form a transcontinental railway system.

Majestic, Mummy, Clay

Literature Anthology,
pages 174–176

? How does the poet use sensory language to describe the demise of the hotel and its role in history.

Talk About It Reread page 175. Talk with a partner about what happened to the hotel and what it's like now.

Cite Text Evidence What words and phrases does the poet use to bring life to the old hotel? Write them in the web.

Tip of the Week

When I **reread**, I pay close attention to the poet's word choice. I find text evidence to answer questions.

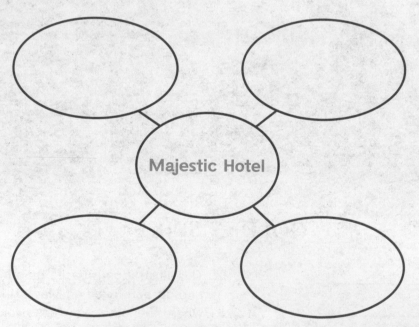

Majestic Hotel

Brianna

Write The poet's use of sensory language helps me see that the hotel _____

_____

_____

SW Productions/Brand X Pictures/Getty Images

? How does the author help you understand the message the poems have in common?

Talk About It Reread "Mummy" and "Clay" on page 176. Talk with a partner about what the two poems have in common.

Cite Text Evidence How do the poets help you understand the message behind their poems? Write text evidence in the chart.

Mummy	Clay

Write The poets help me see the common theme in their poems by _____

_____

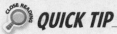 **QUICK TIP**

I can use these sentence frames when we talk about how the poet uses sensory language to share a message.

In "Mummy," the poet . . .

In "Clay," the poet . . .

This helps me understand that the poets . . .

Your Turn

Think about how each poet uses objects to tell about the past. How does that help you understand how they feel? Use these sentence frames to organize your text evidence.

The poets use the hotel, the mummy, and clay to . . .

This tells me . . .

I can see that the poets think the past . . .

Go Digital!
Write your response online.

? How does the poet help you understand the maestro's inspiration?

QUICK TIP

When I reread, I can look at sensory langauge to help me understand what the poet means.

COLLABORATE

Talk About It Reread "Maestro" on page 178. Talk with a partner about the way the poet describes how the maestro's past influences his present.

Cite Text Evidence What phrases does the poet use to describe the maestro's inspiration? Write them in the web.

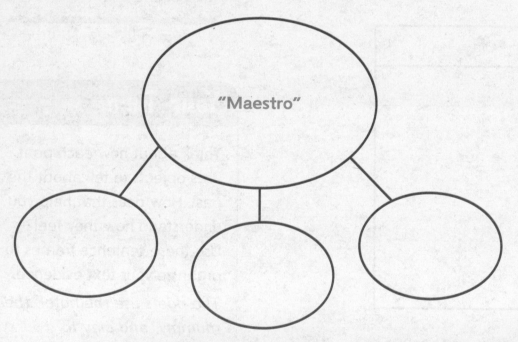

"Maestro"

Write The poet helps me understand the maestro's past influences by _____

_____

_____

? **How do the poets use point of view to set the tone in their poems?**

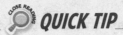 **QUICK TIP**

When I reread, I can focus on point of view to help me understand the tone of the poem.

Talk About It Reread "Maestro" and "Tradition." With a partner, identify the speaker's point of view in each poem and how it affects tone.

Cite Text Evidence What words and phrases help you understand who is speaking and how it affects tone? Write text evidence in the chart.

"Maestro"	"Tradition"	Tone

Write The poets use point of view to develop tone by _____

_____

_____

? How is the way the photographer shows the archaeologist similar to the way the poets use artifacts as inspiration in the poems "Majestic," "Mummy," and "Clay"?

COLLABORATE

Talk About It Look at the photograph and read the caption. Talk with a partner about what each person is doing.

Cite Text Evidence Circle clues in the photograph that help you understand how the archaeologist and the student feel about the bones they are examining. Underline one clue that shows how you know the archaeologist respects what she does.

Write I know that artifacts and objects from the past can

inspire because they _____

_____

_____

_____

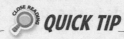
QUICK TIP

I can use details in the photograph to help me understand how important artifacts are. This helps me compare it to the poems I read this week.

Hill Street Studios/Blend Images/Getty Images

An archaeologist shows a skull to a student. The bones are from a museum's storage collection.

How Tía Lola Came to ~~Visit~~ Stay

? How does the author use dialogue to foreshadow what happens later in the story?

COLLABORATE

Talk About It Reread the last paragraph on page 186 and the first paragraph on page 187. Talk about the conversation between Mami and Tía Lola.

Cite Text Evidence What does Tía Lola say that foreshadows what will happen with Colonel Charlebois? Write why it is important in the chart.

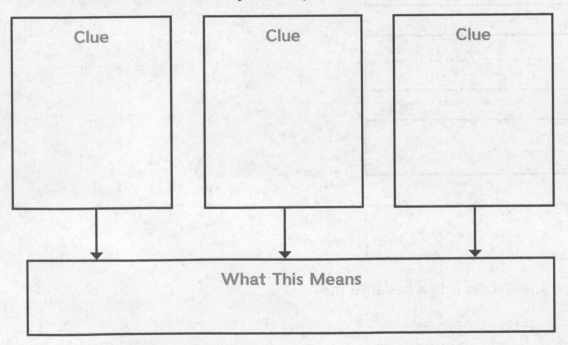

| Clue | Clue | Clue |

What This Means

CLOSE READING **Tip** of the **Week**

When I **reread**, I can think about the author's use of literary elements. I look for clues and evidence in the text.

Michael

Write The author uses dialogue to foreshadow what happens in the story by ___

_____

_____

Lilly Dong/Photodisc/Getty Images

? How do you know that Tía Lola knows more about Colonel Charlebois than any of the other characters?

COLLABORATE

Talk About It Reread the last three paragraphs on page 189. Talk with a partner about Tía Lola's plan and what Mami and Miguel think.

Cite Text Evidence What is the significance of the word *change* in this part of the story? Find text evidence and tell how it helps you understand the plot.

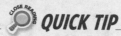 **QUICK TIP**

I can use these sentence frames when we talk about Tía Lola's plan.

The author uses the word change *in different ways to . . .*

This helps me understand Tía Lola's plan because . . .

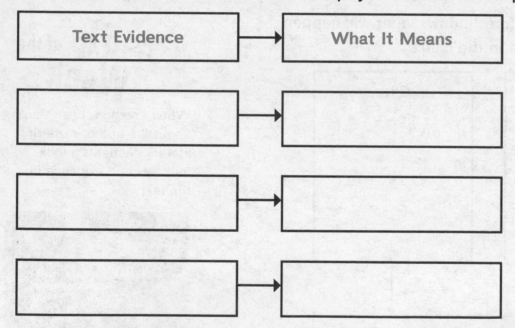

Text Evidence	→	What It Means
	→	
	→	
	→	

Write I know that Tía Lola knows what Colonel Charlebois is like because the author _____

_____

_____

? How does the author help you visualize the change in Colonel Charlebois at the end of the story?

Talk About It Reread the last two paragraphs on page 191. Discuss with a partner what Colonel Charlebois does.

Cite Text Evidence How does the author describe what Colonel Charlebois does when he reads the pennant? Write text evidence in the chart.

Text Evidence	What I Visualize

Write The author helps me visualize the change in Colonel Charlebois by _____

_____

_____

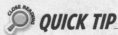

QUICK TIP

When I reread, I can use the author's words to help me visualize how characters change through the story.

Your Turn

Tía Lola knows that Colonel Charlebois will not evict Miguel and his family. How does the author convey Tía's strong feelings? Use these sentence frames to organize your text evidence.

Julia Alvarez paints Tía Lola as . . .

She uses dialogue to . . .

This is important because it helps me. . .

Go Digital!
Write your response online.

The Music of Many

1   One summer morning, a king sat by an open window in his castle. Outside a chorus of birds chirped and warbled together. Each bird had a unique song, but the beautiful sounds blended together in exquisite harmony, delighting the king.

2   Listening to the beautiful birdsong soon became the king's greatest pleasure, and he looked forward to the birds' melodies. Yet in autumn, as the days began to shorten, the birds flew away one by one, leaving silence where their music had once graced the air.

3   The king was saddened by the loss of music. Upon seeing the king's glum face, his most loyal and humble servant said, "Your Majesty, perhaps in winter, a musician could play to while away the quiet." The king agreed, and he ordered his servant to find the most talented musicians in the world.

4   Soon a harpsichordist arrived from England. A sitar player brought his stringed instrument from India. A Peruvian pipe player arrived in a brightly woven shirt, bursting with color. In a short time, musicians from many lands had gathered in the courtyard of the king's castle to audition.

Reread and use the prompts to take notes in the text.

Reread paragraphs 1 and 2. Underline phrases that describe how the king feels about the birds' songs.

Circle the words that tell how the king's feelings change in paragraph 3.

COLLABORATE

Talk with a partner about how the author foreshadows what happens at the end of the allegory. Draw a box around the text evidence that supports your ideas. Write it here:

_____

_____

1　As the sun began to ebb in the late afternoon, the musicians needed to keep warm, so the flutist decided to limber up and began to play a few notes. The drummer beat a slow tap to keep time with the flutist, and then the guitarist from Spain strummed a few chords and the Peruvian pipe player took up the tune and harmonized soulfully. The other musicians joined in.

2　Inside the throne room, the final musician finished her audition, but the king stared into space, dreaming of the birds that had sung so beautifully outside his window.

3　As the king sat, his ears strained to pick up a few notes that wafted through the thick castle walls. A grin slowly crept across the king's face. "At last!" he exclaimed. "That is the sound I have been seeking!" He looked at the members of the court and exclaimed, "Allow me to share an insight I have gained. It is not one sound but the music of many blended together that is truly beautiful."

4　With that, he commanded his servants to invite all of the musicians to enter and form a royal orchestra. Of course, they would have summers off, once the birds returned.

Reread paragraph 2. Circle how you know how the king feels about the musicians who were auditioning. Write what the king does here:

1. _____

2. _____

Talk with a partner about what the king hears. How does the author help you visualize what the king is feeling? Underline text evidence in paragraph 3 to support your discussion.

How does the author help you visualize how the king gains insight about the value of working together?

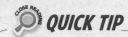

QUICK TIP

When I reread, I can compare and connect the author's ideas throughout the text.

COLLABORATE

Talk About It Reread paragraphs 1 and 2 on page 70. Then, reread paragraph 3 on page 71. Talk with a partner about what the king does.

Cite Text Evidence What clues help you understand how the king realizes the lesson about working together? Record your answers in the chart below.

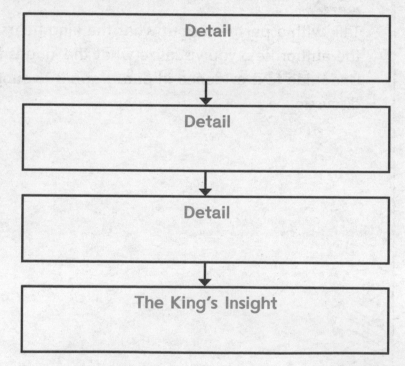

Detail

↓

Detail

↓

Detail

↓

The King's Insight

Write I visualize how the king gains his insight because the author _____

_____

_____

? How does John Milton Hay and the authors of *How Tía Lola Came to Visit* ~~Stay~~ and "The Music of Many" help you understand the impact of words and ideas?

COLLABORATE

Talk About It Read the poem. Talk with a partner about the two ideas that came to the narrator and the effect they had.

Cite Text Evidence Underline the lines in the poem that describe how the narrator got his ideas. Then circle clues that show their impact.

Write I understand the impact words and ideas have because _____

_____

_____

_____

©Ocean/Corbis

Words

When violets were springing
    And sunshine filled the day,
And happy birds were singing
    The praises of the May,
A word came to me, blighting
    The beauty of the scene,
And in my heart was winter,
    Though all the trees were green.

Now down the blast go sailing
    The dead leaves, brown and sere;
The forests are bewailing
    The dying of the year;
A word comes to me, lighting
    With rapture all the air,
And in my heart is summer,
    Though all the trees are bare.

— John Milton Hay

Lizzie Bright and the Buckminster Boy

Literature Anthology,
pages 196–207

 How does the author's use of personification help you visualize the setting as Turner rows the boat?

Talk About It Reread the first paragraph on page 202. Talk with a partner about what the author's words help you picture in your mind.

Cite Text Evidence What two examples of personification help you visualize the setting? Use text evidence to describe the imagery.

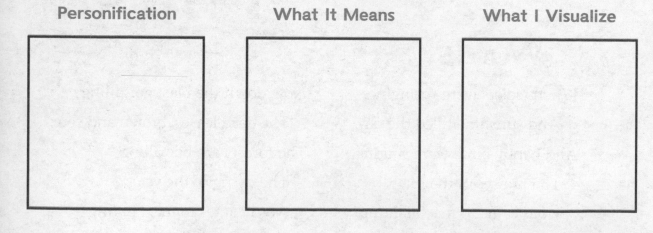

Personification	What It Means	What I Visualize

Write I can visualize the setting because the author uses personification to _____

_____

Kali Nine LLC/iStock/Getty Images

Tip of the **Week**
CLOSE READING

When I **reread**, I look for figurative language, such as personification. I think about the images and feelings the author creates with words.

Evelyn

? How does the author use descriptive language to show how Turner's attitude toward the whale changes?

COLLABORATE

Talk About It Reread page 205. Talk with a partner about how the author describes the encounter between Turner and the whale.

Cite Text Evidence What phrases tell the mood and how does it affect the relationship between Turner and the whale? Write text evidence in the chart.

QUICK TIP

I can use these sentence frames when we talk how the author describes Turner and the whale:

The author describes the encounter between Turner and the whale by . . .

This helps me understand that Turner feels . . .

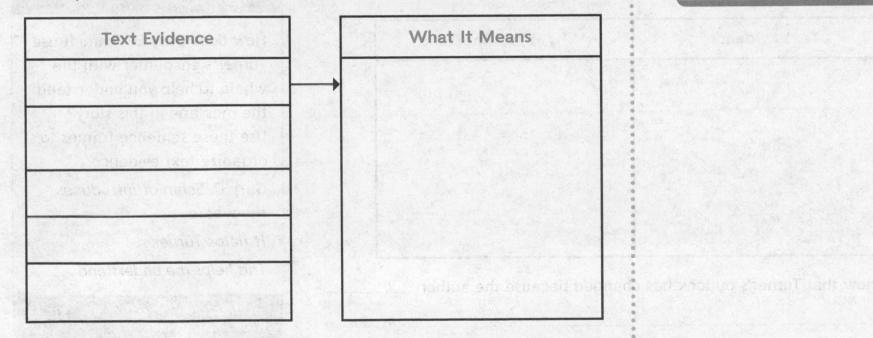

Text Evidence	What It Means

Write The author uses descriptive language to show how Turner changes by ____

_____

_____

How do you know that Turner's outlook has changed?

Talk About It Reread the last four paragraphs on page 207. Talk with a partner about how Turner feels at the end of the story.

Cite Text Evidence What clues show how Turner feels at the end of the story? Record text evidence in the chart.

Text Evidence	Why It Is Important

Write I know that Turner's outlook has changed because the author _____

_____

_____

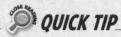 **QUICK TIP**

I can analyze figurative language to learn what the author wants me to understand.

Your Turn

How does Gary D. Schmidt use Turner's encounter with the whale to help you understand the message in this story? Use these sentence frames to organize text evidence.

Gary D. Schmidt introduces the whale . . .

It helps Turner . . .

This helps me understand . . .

Go Digital!
Write your response online.

Confronting a Challenge

1   Even though Ben was very patient, I was so embarrassed by my clumsiness that I began to make up excuses for not skating.

2   About a month later, walking home from school, I discovered a faster route home. It took me past a large pond that was completely frozen over. One day I noticed a woman teaching a young girl to skate. The girl was attempting to jump and spin in the air. Over and over, she pushed off the ground with the toe of her skate. And over and over, she landed hard on the ice.

3   After I had been watching the girl practice for about a week, one Thursday afternoon she suddenly lifted off the ground, spun in the air, and landed on her feet! Her hard work and perseverance had paid off.

4   Later, alone in my bedroom, I started my social studies homework. I read a chapter in my textbook about Robert Peary, a Caucasian man, and Matthew Henson, an African-American, who explored the arctic together in 1909. I could only imagine the fears these explorers had to conquer in order to visit a remote region few people had ever traveled to before.

Scott Altmann

Reread and use the prompts to take notes in the text.

Reread paragraph 1. Circle why the narrator stopped skating. Write it here:

_____

Now underline the clue in paragraph 3 that shows the narrator's attitude was changing.

COLLABORATE

Talk with a partner about why the narrator's attitude was changing. Then reread paragraph 4 and draw a box around two more things that changed the narrator's attitude.

5   When I finished reading I made a pact with myself. The next day I used some money I had earned shoveling snow to buy myself some brand new skates. Every day on the way home from school I stopped at the pond, laced up, and wobbled onto the ice, right next to the figure skater who had landed her jump. As she perfected her twists and tricks, I taught myself to glide and turn. It was hard to fight the urge to simply give up. Instead, every time I went down, I just picked myself up and started over again. If nothing else, I was persistent.

6   Soon I was able to keep my balance and skate more confidently. In just a few weeks, I was actually ready to practice the speed skating, fast stops, and quick turns needed for ice hockey. When I was finally ready to show Ben my newfound skating ability, he was impressed. He told me I should join the local hockey league.

7   I tried out and was chosen for a team. By the end of the season, not only was I part of a winning team, but also I had a group of new friends, including Ben.

In paragraph 5, number the steps the narrator takes to make a change. Underline words and phrases that show how he feels about the process.

Reread paragraph 6. How do you know that the narrator is not going to give up? Circle the text evidence.

COLLABORATE

Reread paragraph 7. Talk with a partner how things have changed for the narrator. Make a mark in the margin beside the clue that helps support your discussion. Write it here:

_____

_____

How does the author show how the narrator changes from the beginning of the story to the end?

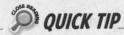
Talk About It Reread paragraphs 1 and 7 on pages 77 and 78. Talk with a partner about how the narrator changes.

Cite Text Evidence How does the author help you understand how the narrator changes? Record text evidence in the chart.

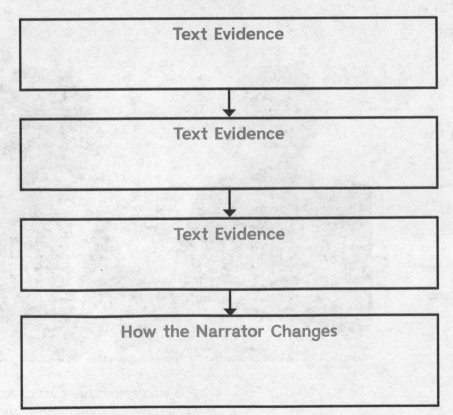

Text Evidence

↓

Text Evidence

↓

Text Evidence

↓

How the Narrator Changes

Write I know that the narrator changes because the author _____

_____

? How does the photographer show the boys' relationship and how does this relationship compare to the ones in *Lizzie Bright and the Buckminster Boy* and "Confronting a Challenge"?

COLLABORATE

Talk About It With a partner, discuss how each boy in the photograph is helping the other to overcome challenges. Compare them to Turner and the whale and the narrator and the figure skater.

Cite Text Evidence Look at the photograph. Work with a partner to find and circle three clues that show how the interaction between the boys is benefitting them. List the ways in the margin beside the photograph. Draw a box around clues that show how the boys feel.

Write The boys in the photograph are like Turner and the narrator because _____

_____

_____

_____

_____

QUICK TIP

I see the boys are building a relationship. This will help me compare the photograph with the stories I read this week.

fatihhoca/Vetta/Getty Images

These sixth graders are part of their school's new One-on-One mentoring program. The program pairs two students with different talents who mentor and work together for one hour a week.

The Pot That Juan Built

Literature Anthology, pages 212–223

? How does the author help you understand how Juan was inspired to create his pottery using only local materials?

COLLABORATE

Talk About It Reread page 217. Talk about how Juan found his inspiration to create pottery.

Cite Text Evidence What clues help you figure out why Juan uses only local materials? Record your text evidence in the chart.

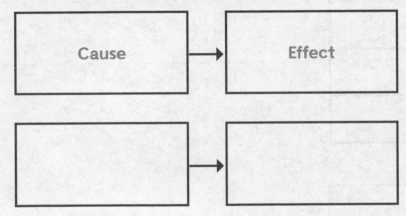

Cause	→	Effect
	→	

Write The author helps me understand how Juan was inspired to use local materials by _____

_____

CLOSE READING **Tip** of the **Week**

When I **reread**, I think about how the author uses descriptive words to tell about a character's motivation. I find text evidence to answer questions.

Dena

©Nicole Hill/Rubberball/Corbis

How does the author's use of details help you visualize how Juan gets his materials?

Talk About It Reread page 218. Talk about how Juan collects what he needs to polish his pots.

Cite Text Evidence What words and phrases show what Juan uses to polish his clay pots? Write them in the chart and tell how it helps you visualize.

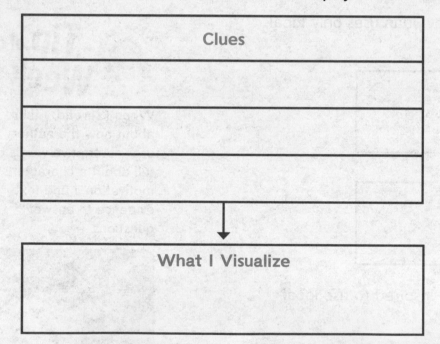

Clues

↓

What I Visualize

Write I can visualize how Juan gets the materials he needs because the author

_____

_____

? How does the author help you understand how Juan feels about his pottery?

COLLABORATE

Talk About It Reread page 223. Talk with a partner about Juan's comments about his pottery and how it has affected Mata Ortiz.

Cite Text Evidence What clues help you understand how Juan feels? Record text evidence in the chart below.

Text Evidence	How Juan Feels

Write The author helps me understand how Juan feels about his pottery by

_____

_____

_____

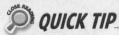

QUICK TIP

When I reread, I can use the way the author shares information to better understand what the text means.

Your Turn

How does the author help you understand how local people, plants, animals, and earth are important to Juan's pottery? Use these sentence frames to organize your text evidence.

The author describes Juan as . . .

Juan creates pottery using. . .

This is important because . . .

Go Digital!
Write your response online.

A Box of Ideas

Scene 1

1. **Chris** *(watching Ms. Cerda)*: What's that box you're making?

2. **Ms. Cerda:** It's called a nicho. This one celebrates my mother. First, I made a tin box. Then I punched out a design using a hammer and a tool called an awl, which is like a thick nail, but not so sharp. See how the dots look like a flower? It's a dahlia, my mother's favorite.

3. **Chris:** It's Mexico's national flower, too.

4. **Ms. Cerda:** That's right, it is.

5. **Inés** *(laughing)*: Hey, Chris! Stop pestering my mom.

6. **Gil:** I told you he was too young to help out.

7. **Silvia:** We could do a car wash.

8. **Inés:** No way! My hands are still peeling from the last one.

Reread and use the prompts to take notes in the text.

Reread lines 1 and 2. Circle what Ms. Cerda's purpose is for making her nicho. Then number the steps she describes to Chris. Write the numbers in the margin.

Talk with a partner about why the author includes directions about how to make a nicho. Reread lines 5 and 6. How is the author hinting what will happen later in the play? Underline the clue and write it here:

_____

Scene 2

Setting: The School Fair, three weeks later

1. *(Inés, Silvia, Gil, and Chris stand behind a table with a hand-painted sign that says, "Neighborhood Nichos." There is one nicho on the table. Ms. Cerda comes by, picks up the nicho, and looks inside.)*

2. **Ms. Cerda:** I'm impressed. You've all become expert nicho makers. This is beautiful.

3. **Inés:** I got the shoebox from you, mom!

4. **Silvia:** I added the doors – they came from a grocery story carton.

5. **Gil:** That one celebrates Main Street. I took pictures of the stores and cars. My uncle printed them out for us.

6. **Chris:** I got some wire for the tree trunks from Mr. Marsalis, the electrician next door. The treetops are made of green yarn that Ms. Miller gave us.

7. **Inés:** And I added bottle caps to make the car tires.

8. **Ms. Cerda:** Very clever. I'm really impressed by your ingenuity.

Reread line 1. Draw a box around where the author tells you the setting has changed.

Reread lines 3–8. Circle how Inés, Silvia, Gil, and Chris contributed to the neighborhood nicho.

COLLABORATE

Talk with a partner about how Chris got the idea to make nichos. Then use your annotations to discuss how the students got the neighborhood involved. Use text evidence to write your response here:

_____

_____

_____

_____

_____

Why is "A Box of Ideas" a good title for this selection?

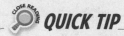 **QUICK TIP**

When I reread drama, I think about what each person says and how it helps me understand the characters' actions.

COLLABORATE

Talk About It Reread the excerpts on pages 84 and 85. Talk with a partner about what a nicho is and what the conversation between Chris and Ms. Cerda leads to.

Cite Text Evidence What clues help you understand how Ms. Cerda's nicho was the inspiration for the neighborhood nichos? Write evidence in the chart.

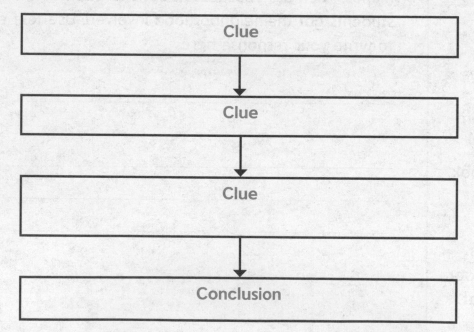

Clue

↓

Clue

↓

Clue

↓

Conclusion

Write "A Box of Ideas" is a good title for this selection because _____

_____

_____

_____

? How do the songwriter's lyrics and the authors' words and phrases in *The Pot That Juan Built* and "A Box of Ideas" help you understand the theme of collaboration?

Library of Congress Prints and Photographs Division (LC-USZ62-990521)

Talk About It Read the song lyrics. Talk with a partner about what it means to "push the business on." Discuss the theme of the song.

Cite Text Evidence Circle the text evidence in the lyrics that describe how the narrators will work to move their goods. Underline how they will make the business better.

Write All three authors help me understand theme by _____

_____

_____

_____

_____

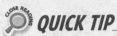

QUICK TIP
I use the lyrics to help me understand the theme. This helps me compare the song with the stories I read this week.

Push the Business On

We'll hire a horse and grab a rig;

And all the world will dance a jig;

And we will do whatever we can to push the business on.

To push the business on.

To push the business on.

And we will do whatever we can to push the business on.

Major Taylor: Champion Cyclist

Why does the author include fictional details in the dialogue between Marshall and Mr. Hay?

Literature Anthology, pages 230–243

COLLABORATE

Talk About It Reread the dialogue on page 232. Talk about what you learn about Mr. Hay and Marshall.

Cite Text Evidence What are the fictional details in the biography? Cite text evidence to tell the author's purpose.

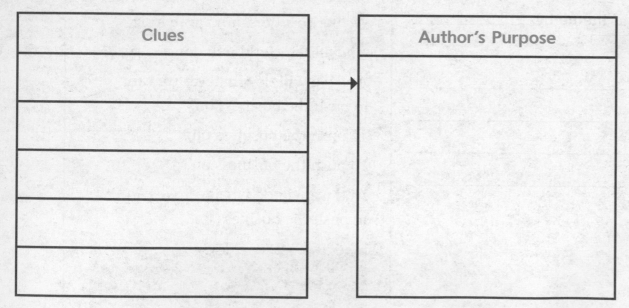

Clues	Author's Purpose

Tip of the Week

CLOSE READING

When I **reread**, I can think about how the author uses fictional details in a biography. I look for text evidence to answer questions.

Daniel

Purestock/SuperStock

Write The author includes fictional details in this biography _____

_____

? How does the author help you visualize how the other riders felt about Marshall?

Talk About It Reread the last paragraph on page 238. Talk with a partner about what you picture in your mind.

Cite Text Evidence What clues help you visualize how some of the other riders treated Marshall? Record evidence from the text.

 QUICK TIP

I can use these sentence frames when we talk about how the other riders felt:

The author uses descriptive language to . . .

It helps me visualize how . . .

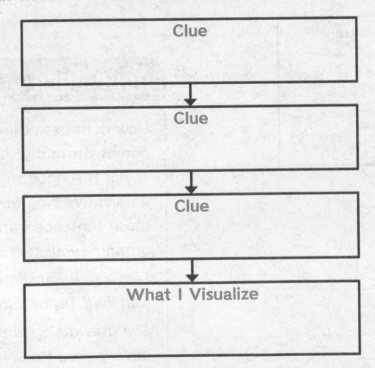

Clue
Clue
Clue
What I Visualize

Write I can visualize how the other riders felt about Marshall because the author

_____

_____

_____

? How do you know that Marshall's victory lap was more than just a win for him?

Talk About It Reread the last paragraph on page 243. Talk with a partner about the significance of the American flag during Marshall's victory lap.

Cite Text Evidence What clues help you understand that what Marshall does with the American flag is important? Write text evidence in the chart.

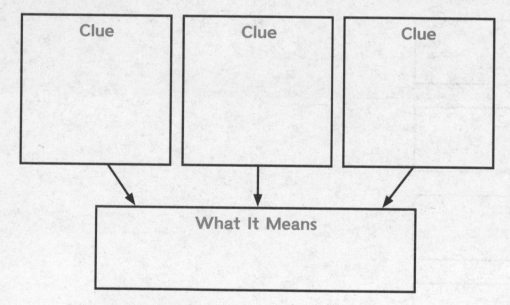

Clue

Clue

Clue

What It Means

Write The author helps me understand that Marshall's victory lap is _____

_____

_____

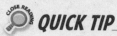

QUICK TIP

When I reread, I use the author's words to visualize and think about the message being presented.

Your Turn

How does Lesa Cline-Ransome demonstrate that Marshall Taylor is a good subject for a narrative biography? Use these sentence frames to organize your text evidence.

Lesa Cline-Ransome tells Marshall Taylor's story by . . .

She uses dialogue and strong descriptions to . . .

This helps me understand that . . .

Go Digital!
Write your response online.

Margaret Bourke-White: Fearless Photographer

[1]   In 1904, girls weren't supposed to dream of careers that took them flying into the sky on airplanes, or climbing out onto ledges at the top of skyscrapers. And they certainly weren't encouraged to think about competing with men for the opportunity to photograph important people and events.

[2]   Joseph White and Minnie Bourke, however, never told their daughter what to think and dream about. Instead, young Margaret, or "Peg" as her friends called her, got plenty of attention and encouragement from her parents to explore her world. Early on, they taught her to work hard and to go after what she wanted. They even gave her a motto: "You can." It's no wonder Margaret Bourke-White grew up to be one of the most accomplished women and talked-about photographers of the twentieth century.

Reread and use the prompts to take notes in the text.

Underline how the author uses foreshadowing in paragraph 1. How do you know that he is referring to Margaret Bourke-White? Write the clue here:

_____

_____

_____

COLLABORATE

Talk with a partner about how Margaret's parents encouraged her. Circle clues in paragraph 2 that support your answer.

How does the author organize the text to make it more interesting to read?

_____

_____

_____

A Lasting Influence

[1]   During the 1930s and 1940s, Margaret's adventurous attitude and perseverance paved the way for women to take on roles beyond the norm. Rather than snapping photos of high-society parties as other female photographers had done before her, she marched into steel plants and combat zones. She proved to women that they had every right to pursue the careers they wanted.

[2]   Through her work, Margaret became a role model for working women as well as a strong voice for the poor and powerless. She earned the respect of powerful businessmen when women were discouraged from working. When she died in 1971, she left behind not only an amazing photographic record of the human experience. She also left a message for women all over the world who wanted to make an impact: "You can."

Reread the excerpt. Circle five words or phrases that the author uses to help you understand the kind of person Margaret was. Write them here:

1. _____

2. _____

3. _____

4. _____

5. _____

   _____

COLLABORATE

Talk with a partner about the way Margaret's achievements helped women. Draw boxes around clues in paragraph 2 that support your discussion.

? **Why does the author begin and end the selection with the phrase "You Can"?**

COLLABORATE

Talk About It Reread paragraph 2 on both pages 91 and 92. Talk with a partner about the author's use of repetition.

Cite Text Evidence What clues show why the author repeats Margaret's motto? Find text evidence and write what the author wants you to know.

Beginning	End	What It Means

Write The author begins and ends the selection with "You Can" because _____

_____

_____

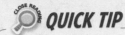
QUICK TIP

When I reread, I can analyze why the author uses repetition.

? How does Robert Cornelius's milestone in photography compare with the way the authors of *Major Taylor: Champion Cyclist* and "Margaret Bourke-White: Fearless Photographer" describe the contributions of the people in their selections?

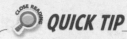

QUICK TIP

I can use clues in the photograph and caption to help me compare it to text.

COLLABORATE

Talk About It Look at the photograph and read the caption. Talk with a partner about what Robert Cornelius is doing in this photograph. Discuss how this compares with what Marshall Taylor and Margaret Bourke-White did.

Cite Text Evidence Circle a clue in the self-portrait that helps you understand how Robert Cornelius felt about his achievement. Underline text evidence in the caption that supports how one person can change other peoples' opinions.

Write Robert Cornelius's self-portrait is like _____

_____

_____

Robert Cornelius took this photograph of himself in 1839. It is believed to be the first self-portrait ever taken.

Stewards of the Environment

? Why does the author begin the selection with information about President Theodore Roosevelt?

Literature Anthology, pages 250–253

COLLABORATE

Talk About It Reread the first two paragraphs on page 251. Talk with a partner about Theodore Roosevelt's conservation efforts.

Cite Text Evidence How does the author transition from the work Roosevelt did to what conservationists are doing today? Record text evidence in the chart.

Text Evidence	What It Means

Write The author begins the selection with information about President Roosevelt to _____

_____

Tip of the Week

CLOSE READING

When I **reread**, I think about how ideas are connected. I find text evidence to answer questions.

Fatima

© Zurijeta/iStock/Getty Images

? How does the author use text features to help you understand how important recycling is?

COLLABORATE

Talk About It Reread page 253. Talk with a partner about what it takes to start a recycling program.

Cite Text Evidence How does the organization of the information help you understand it better? Use this chart to record text evidence.

Flow Chart	Photograph and Caption	How It Helps

Write The author uses text features to help me _____

_____

Your Turn

How does the author feel about people who work to address environmental problems? Use these sentence frames to organize your text evidence.

The author begins the selection with . . .

He shares his opinion by . . .

This helps me understand . . .

Go Digital!
Write your response online.

Modern Transit for an Ancient City

1   In September 1997, the city of Athens, Greece, won the honor of hosting the 2004 summer Olympic Games. A key factor in the decision was the city's promise to have a modern metro (subway) system ready to serve people who came to the games. Most people who live in cities around the world are advocates of mass transit. Busses and trains move large numbers of people while minimizing the use of fossil fuels. Even a city as ancient as Athens can and should have a "green" mass transit system, Olympics or no Olympics.

2   Greece has a population of over 10.5 million people. Nearly half of them are crowded into the city of Athens. Before 1994, polluting emissions from cars and other vehicles were completely unregulated. Athens was frequently shrouded in smog. The dirty air was unhealthy for people, and it was damaging the ancient cultural treasures of Greece, including the Parthenon and other monuments.

Reread and use the prompts to take notes in the text.

Underline the sentence in paragraph 1 that states the author's argument. Reread paragraph 2. Circle words and phrases that describe Athens before mass transit.

COLLABORATE

Talk with a partner about how the author feels about mass transit. Use text evidence to support your response. Write it here:

_____

_____

_____

_____

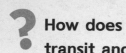

? How does the author use descriptive language to help you visualize mass transit and understand his perspective?

COLLABORATE

Talk About It Reread the excerpt on page 97. Talk with a partner about how the author describes mass transit.

Cite Text Evidence What clues help you understand the author's perspective on mass transit? Record text evidence in the chart.

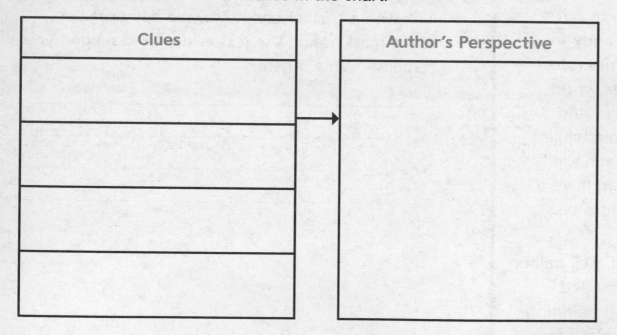

Clues	Author's Perspective

Write The author reveals his perspective of mass transit by _____

_____

_____

QUICK TIP

When I reread, I can use the author's words to help me understand his perspective.

? How does the way the photographer frames Lingang New City compare with the way the authors organize text in "Stewards of the Environment" and "Modern Transit for an Ancient City"?

George Hammerstein/Corbis/Glow Images

COLLABORATE

Talk About It Look at the photograph and read the caption. Talk with a partner about what you see. Discuss why the photographer used this angle to photograph Lingang New City.

Cite Text Evidence Circle clues in the photograph that help you see what the photographer thinks is important. Underline evidence in the caption that supports what the photographer wants you to know.

Write The photographer and authors organize their information to help me _____

_____

_____

CLOSE READING
QUICK TIP
When I look at a photograph, I can compare it to what I've read about other environments.

This residential area in Lingang New City, China, features rows of apartment buildings with rooftop solar panels. Lingang New City is a trial "green city" that relies on solar power for all its energy and will feature energy-saving technology and only electric cars and ferries.

Years of Dust:
The Story of the Dust Bowl

How does the author use sidebars to help you understand how extreme weather on the plains can be?

Literature Anthology:
pages 256–271

Talk About It Reread the sidebar on page 259. Talk with a partner about what winter was like on the plains.

Cite Text Evidence What phrases describe the severity of winter on the plains? Write text evidence in the chart.

Text Evidence	Winter on the Plains

Write The author uses a sidebar to help me understand the severity of winter

by _____

_____

_____

Tip of the **Week**

When I **reread**, I can use text features to help me understand the topic. I look for text evidence to answer questions.

Ben

Radius Images/Alamy

? How does the author use descriptive details to help you understand the importance of the buffalo to the Great Plains?

COLLABORATE

Talk About It Reread the first two paragraphs on page 263. Talk with a partner about how the author uses the word *keystone*.

Cite Text Evidence What information shows that the buffalo were crucial to the survival of the Great Plains? Write text evidence in the chart.

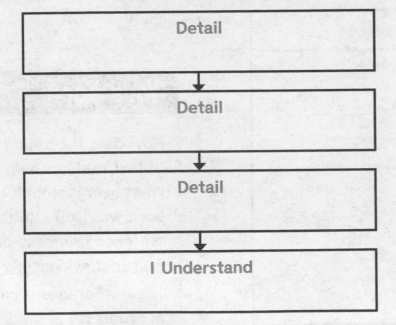

Detail

↓

Detail

↓

Detail

↓

I Understand

Write I understand how important the buffalo were to the Great Plains because

the author _____

_____

_____

? What does the author achieve by using an eyewitness account in this selection?

COLLABORATE

Talk About It Reread page 270. Talk with a partner about what it must have been like to see a dust storm.

Cite Text Evidence What details in A.D. Kirk's account of an approaching dust storm help you understand what it was like? Write text evidence in the chart.

Text Evidence	Inference

Write The author uses the eyewitness account so that I can _____

_____

_____

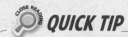 **QUICK TIP**

When I reread, I can use first-person accounts to help me understand a historical event.

Your Turn

How does the author's use of text features help explain what living through the dust bowl was like? Use these sentence frames to organize your text evidence.

The author uses eyewitness accounts to . . .

He also uses text features to explain . . .

This helps me visualize . . .

Go Digital!
Write your response online.

Erica Fernandez: Environmental Activist

1   Erica was barely into her teens when she arrived in California from Mexico with her parents. Not long afterward, Erica found out that a liquefied natural gas facility was being planned for the coast of Oxnard and Malibu. It would include a three-foot wide pipeline that would run through low-income neighborhoods.

2   The result, Erica learned, would be a calamity for the area. Some people estimated that the facility would spew hundreds of tons of pollutants into the air and waters of nearby coastal towns each year.

3   Erica was outraged, and she soon began to mobilize youth, kids her own age and older, because she knew the pipeline would affect their future. Soon over 300 students from neighboring schools were knocking on doors and handing out flyers.

Reread and use the prompts to take notes in the text.

Circle details in paragraph 1 that tell you who Erica was.

Reread paragraph 2. Underline text evidence that helps you understand how the facility would affect people who lived in the area.

COLLABORATE

Reread paragraph 3. How does Erica feel? Draw a box around the clue. Talk with a partner about how that feeling drove her to take action. Make a note in the margin beside what Erica got kids to do.

Why did Erica take action? Circle the text evidence and write it here:

_____

_____

1   By the time two different state commissions met to discuss the project, other large environmental organizations had joined the fight. Next, Erica helped launch a mail and phone call campaign to the governor. After receiving thousands of postcards and phone calls, the governor declared that there would be no pipeline in Oxnard or Malibu.

2   In 2007, Erica's passion and tenacity were rewarded when she was selected as one of six young people to receive the Brower Youth Award. Each year this award is given to students in recognition for their work on behalf of the environment. Young people between the ages of 13 and 22 are eligible for the award.

Reread paragraph 1. Underline how you know that Erica's efforts were getting noticed. Write them here.

1. _____

2. _____

   _____

COLLABORATE

Reread paragraph 2. Talk with a partner about how the author shows how she feels about Erica. Circle text evidence that supports your discussion.

Indrajit Das

? **How do you know how the author feels about Erica Hernandez?**

COLLABORATE

Talk About It Reread paragraph 2 on page 104. Talk with a partner about how the author describes Erica's accomplishments.

Cite Text Evidence What words show how the author feels about Erica? Write text evidence in the chart and how it helps you figure out the author's point of view.

Text Evidence	Author's Point of View

Write I know how the author feels about Erica Hernandez because she _____

_____

_____

? How does the photographer show how people overcome environmental challenges in a similar way as the authors of *Years of Dust: The Story of the Dust Bowl* and "Erica Fernandez, Environmental Activist"?

COLLABORATE

Talk About It With a partner, look at the photograph and read the caption. Discuss the challenges the Uros people have to overcome every day.

Cite Text Evidence Make a mark in the margin beside the photograph that indicates a challenge the Uros people face. Circle three examples of how they overcome this challenge. Then underline text evidence in the caption that helps you understand how the Uros live.

Write Just as Erica Fernandez and the people of *Years of Dust,* the Uros people must _____

_____

_____

_____

_____

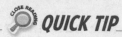
QUICK TIP

I can see that the Uros people have many challenges. This will help me compare the photograph with the selections I read this week.

Glow Images

The Uros people in the photograph live on Lake Titicaca Puno in Peru. They use reeds that grow plentifully around the lake to build the islands, boats, their homes, and almost everything they need.

Seeing Things His Own Way

 ? How does the author's use of Erik's quote help you understand his character?

Literature Anthology:
pages 276–287

Talk About It Reread paragraph 4 on page 278. Talk with a partner about what Erik's quote means.

Cite Text Evidence What does Erik say that helps you understand his character? Write text evidence in the chart and tell why the author uses it.

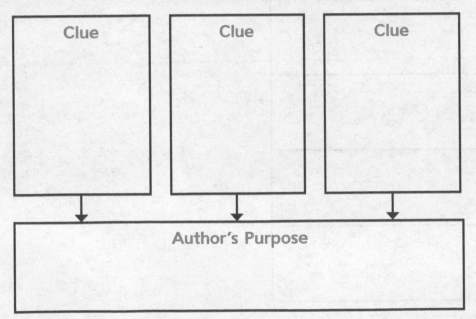

Clue	Clue	Clue

↓ ↓ ↓

Author's Purpose

Write The author uses Erik's quote to help me understand that Erik is _____

_____

_____

CLOSE READING
Tip of the Week

When I **reread**, I can think about how the author uses quotations. I look for text evidence to answer questions.

María

Phillip Spears/Stockbyte/Getty Images

? How do you know that Erik's father played a big role in helping him achieve success in life?

COLLABORATE

Talk About It Reread the last two paragraphs on page 281. Talk with a partner about what Erik's father did after his mother died.

Cite Text Evidence What words and phrases describe what Erik's father did to help Erik succeed? Write text evidence in the chart.

Text Evidence	Conclusion

Write I know that Erik's father played a big role in helping Erik succeed because the author _____

_____

 **QUICK TIP**

I can use these sentence frames when we talk about what Erik's father did.

The author helps me understand what Erik's father did by . . .

This shows that he . . .

? How does the author use descriptive language to help you visualize what mountain climbing was like for Erik?

COLLABORATE

Talk About It Reread the second paragraph on page 284. Talk with a partner about how Erik describes his climb on Mt. Rainier in 1985.

Cite Text Evidence What words and phrases tell about one of Erik's mountain climbing experiences? Write text evidence in the chart.

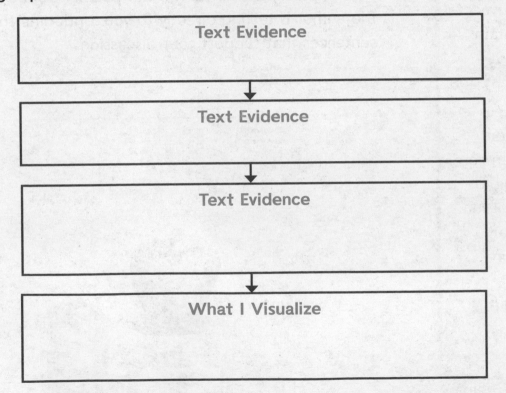

Text Evidence

↓

Text Evidence

↓

Text Evidence

↓

What I Visualize

Write The author uses descriptive language to help me visualize Erik's climb by

_____

_____

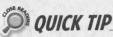

QUICK TIP

When I reread, I think about how the author uses examples to support what he is saying.

Your Turn

How does Marty Kaminsky convince you that Erik should be seen as a role model? Use these sentence frames to organize your text evidence.
Marty Kaminsky uses quotes to show . . .

He shares information about Erik's father to . . .

This makes it clear that . . .

Go Digital!
Write your response online.

Get Fit For Fun!

What Is Fitness?

[1]   Nearly everyone can get into better shape with very little effort.

[2]   There are three main things you should do to be fit. First, it's important to be physically active. Second, eat a healthful diet. And third, maintain a healthy weight for your age and body type. It doesn't matter what your friends weigh!

[3]   As any athlete will tell you, there are degrees of fitness. You can probably walk a mile without getting winded, but could you run a mile? Can you climb several flights of stairs without stopping to catch your breath? Do you think you might eat too much junk food, such as chips, candy, or sugary sodas? Professional athletes must pay attention to diet and exercise to perform at their best, but nearly everybody can increase their regular physical activity and eat a balanced diet.

Reread and use the prompts to take notes in the text.

Reread paragraphs 1 and 2. In the margin beside the text evidence, number the three things you can do to be fit. Circle the sentence that those clues support.

COLLABORATE

Reread paragraph 3. Talk with a partner about why the author is talking directly to you. Underline the sentences that support your discussion.

Your Need for Water

1   Is all this talk of exercise making you thirsty? That's a good thing. In addition to a balanced diet, your body needs water to work properly. You use water to digest your food, to carry nutrients through your blood, to remove waste products, and to cool you through sweating.

Getting Started

2   It's easy to implement a fitness routine. Step away from the remote. Click off the computer. Get off the couch and get moving. Find an exercise buddy. And think about what to eat before you eat it.

3   How can you assess whether you're on the road to fitness?

In paragraph 1, circle what the author does to make the information more interesting to read. Underline text evidence that tells why you need water.

COLLABORATE

Talk with a partner about how the headings help you understand more about what you are reading.

Reread paragraphs 2 and 3. Why is "Getting Started" a good heading? Make marks in the margin beside text evidence that supports your answer. Write why here.

_____

_____

_____

_____

How does the author organize information to help you understand how she feels about fitness?

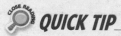

COLLABORATE

Talk About It Reread the excerpt on page 111. Talk with a partner about how the author feels about fitness.

Cite Text Evidence What words and phrases help you understand how the author feels about fitness? Write text evidence in the chart.

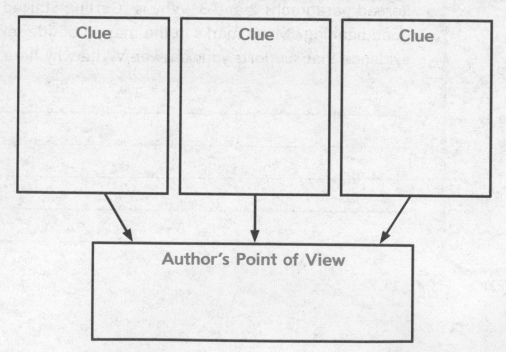

Clue

Clue

Clue

Author's Point of View

Write The author helps me understand how she feels about fitness by _____

_____

_____

? How does the way the poet and the authors of *Seeing Things His Own Way* and "Get Fit For Fun" use words and phrases to help you visualize the theme or message?

Talk About It The word *invictus* is a Latin word meaning unconquered or invincible. Read the poem. Talk with a partner about why this is a good title for the poem.

Cite Text Evidence Underline words and phrases in the poem that help you visualize how the narrator deals with the challenges he faces. Circle how the narrator feels about his challenges and himself.

Write The poet and authors use words and phrases to help me visualize

_____

_____

_____

_____

_____

QUICK TIP

In the poem I read how the narrator overcomes a challenge. This will help me compare it to the selections I read this week.

Invictus

Out of the night that covers me,
Black as the pit from pole to pole,
I thank whatever gods may be
For my unconquerable soul.

In the fell clutch of circumstance
I have not winced nor cried aloud.
Under the bludgeonings of chance
My head is bloody, but unbowed.

Beyond this place of wrath and tears
Looms but the Horror of the shade,
And yet the menace of the years
Finds and shall find me unafraid.

It matters not how strait the gate,
How charged with punishments the scroll,
I am the master of my fate,
I am the captain of my soul.

— William Ernest Henley

The Case of the Magic Marker Mischief Maker

 How do the stage directions impact how you feel about Mickey?

Talk About It Reread the stage directions on page 295. Talk with a partner about what Mickey does and how he acts.

Cite Text Evidence What do the stage directions tell you about what Mickey is like? Write text evidence and explain how it makes you feel about him.

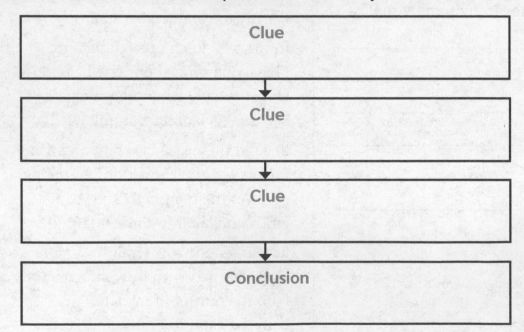

Clue
↓
Clue
↓
Clue
↓
Conclusion

Write The stage directions help me to _____

_____

Literature Anthology: pages 294–303

CLOSE READING

Tip of the Week

When I **reread** a play, I can use stage directions to help me understand the characters. I look for text evidence to answer questions.

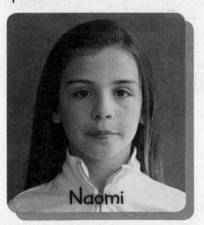

Naomi

? **How does the author use what the characters say to create conflict?**

COLLABORATE

Talk About It Reread the first column on page 296. Talk with a partner about the conversation between Mickey and Principal Abrego.

Cite Text Evidence What words does the author use to show conflict between the characters? Write text evidence in the chart.

Text Evidence	How It Shows Conflict

Write The author uses what the characters say to create conflict by _____

_____

_____

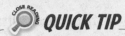
QUICK TIP

I can use these sentence frames when we talk about conflict.

Principal Abrego and Mickey . . .

The author creates conflict by . . .

? How does the author use what Bucho says to help you understand his character?

Talk About It Reread Act Two, Scene 2 on page 300. Talk with a partner about what you learned about Bucho's personality from what he says.

Cite Text Evidence What words and phrases help you know what Bucho is like? Write text evidence in the chart.

What Bucho Says	What It Shows

Write The author helps me understand what Bucho is like by _____

_____

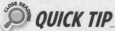

QUICK TIP
When I reread, I can use dialogue to help me understand what the characters do.

Your Turn

How does the author use conflict to help you understand the decisions Mickey makes? Use these sentence frames to organize your thoughts.

The author uses stage directions to . . .

He helps me understand that Mickey and Bucho . . .

I see that Mickey's decisions . . .

Go Digital!
Write your response online.

Dramatic Decisions:
Theater Through the Ages

Kabuki Theater

1　On the other side of the world at about the same time, another new theatrical style was developing in Japan. Called "kabuki," it began in the early 1600s with female casts. Soon, however, the actors were all males. Kabuki performances entail extravagant makeup and costumes and include dancing and singing.

2　One of the greatest kabuki playwrights is Chikamatsu Monzaemon. His play *Sonezaki Shinju*, which was published in 1720, has a plot that is similar to *Romeo and Juliet*. In it two young people are in love, but circumstances prevent them from being together. Audiences identify with them as they unsuccessfully try to follow their hearts and make a desperate decision to escape together.

Reread and use the prompts to take notes in the text.

Circle how you know what the first paragraph is about. Write it here.

_____

_____

Underline clues in paragraph 1 that describe Kabuki.

Reread paragraph 2. Talk with a partner about how the author helps you understand what the play *Sonezaki Shinju* is about. Make marks in the margin beside text evidence that supports your discussion.

Modern American Theater

3   In 1736, the Dock Street Theatre in Charles-Towne, South Carolina – now called Charleston– was built. It was the first building in the North American colonies erected solely to be a theater. Today, actors perform in theaters everywhere across the country, from the great stages of New York to small community theaters. But some aspects of the experience have never changed, including the popularity of plays in which characters are faced with difficult decisions to make.

4   One very popular modern American play is *A Raisin in the Sun* by Lorraine Hansberry. The play centers on the Youngers, an African-American family on the South Side of Chicago. Set in the 1950s, the story dramatizes the difficult choice faced by the family, which is about to receive a large sum of money. The adult Youngers have different ideas about what to do with the money. Each person's idea is valid, but each has a different goal—and it excludes the others. In the end, decisions are made and problems are resolved as the characters hoped they would be.

In paragraph 3, circle one aspect of the theater experience that is common to all theaters.

Reread paragraph 4. Underline how the author helps you see that this is true.

COLLABORATE

Talk with a partner about what *A Raisin in the Sun* is about. Why does the author use this play as an example in the section "Modern American Theater?" Make marks in the margin to show text evidence that supports your answer.

? **How does the way the author organizes information help you understand the history of theater?**

Talk About It Reread the excerpts on pages 118 and 119. Talk about one way the author helps you understand how theater came to be.

Cite Text Evidence How does the author organize the information? Write text evidence to support how it helps you understand the topic.

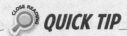 **QUICK TIP**

When I reread, I can use the way the author organizes text to help me understand the topic.

Text Evidence

↓

How It Helps

Write The author helps me understand the history of theater by _____

_____

? How are difficult decisions portrayed by the photographer and the authors of *The Case of the Magic Marker Mischief Maker* and "Dramatic Decisions: Theater Through the Ages"?

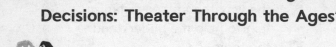

COLLABORATE

Talk About It Look at the photograph and read the caption. Talk with a partner about what you see happening in the photograph. Identify the people and discuss each person's role.

Cite Text Evidence Circle clues in the photograph that show how performers work through their decisions about how to portray characters on stage. Draw a box around two things that help them reach a decision about what to do. Underline evidence in the caption that supports your answer.

Write The way the photographer shows how people resolve difficult decisions is like _____

_____

_____

_____

_____

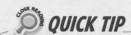

QUICK TIP

I see in the photograph how decisions must be made in order for the actors to portray believable characters. This will help me compare it to the selections I read this week.

Rayman/Photodisc/Getty Images

The actors in this theatre group rehearse a scene from their upcoming play. The play's director helps them decide how each actor should portray the characters.

Home of the Brave

How does the author organize the text to help you understand what Kek experiences on his first day of school?

Talk About It Reread the left column on page 312. Talk with a partner about what Kek is saying and what he is thinking.

Cite Text Evidence How do you know how Kek is telling his story? Write text evidence in the chart.

Kek Tells	Kek Thinks

Write The author organizes the text to help me understand what Kek

experiences by _____

_____

CLOSE READING

Tip of the Week

When I **reread**, I use the character's point of view to help me understand the events in the story. I look for text evidence to answer questions.

Leah

? **How do you know that Ms. Hernandez and Mr. Franklin understand how Kek is feeling?**

COLLABORATE

Talk About It Reread page 314. Turn and talk to a partner about what Ms. Hernandez and Mr. Franklin talk about to Kek.

Cite Text Evidence What words and phrases show that Ms. Hernandez and Mr. Franklin understand how Kek is feeling? Write text evidence in the chart.

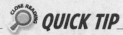 **QUICK TIP**

I can use these sentence frames when we talk about the characters.

The author shows that the teachers . . .

This helps me understand that they . . .

Text Evidence	What It Means

Write I know that Ms. Hernandez and Mr. Franklin understand how Kek feels

because the author _____

_____

_____

How does the author use Kek's limited English vocabulary to help you understand how he feels about lunchtime?

COLLABORATE

Talk About It Reread page 317. Talk with a partner about how Kek describes lunch in the cafeteria.

Cite Text Evidence What words and phrases paint a picture of what happens at lunchtime? Write text evidence here.

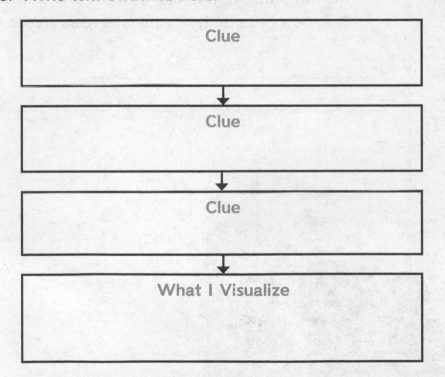

Clue

↓

Clue

↓

Clue

↓

What I Visualize

Write The author uses Kek's limited vocabulary to describe lunchtime by _____

_____

_____

 QUICK TIP

When I reread, I can use a character's words and phrases to understand how he feels.

Your Turn

How does the author use Kek's interior monologue to help you understand the story's theme? Use these sentence frames to organize your text evidence.

The author describes Kek as . . .

Kek's interior monologue tells me that . . .

This helps me understand that Kek . . .

Go Digital!
Write your response online.

Aminata's Tale

1   "*Moi?*" Aminata asked, pointing to herself. Did Ms. Simpson really expect her to stand in front of the class and tell them how she had come to this country?

2   When Ms. Simpson nodded, a rush of hot terror burned in Aminata's stomach and seemed to dash down to her toes, paralyzing her on the spot. She had been in the United States only a short time and barely knew any words in English. How could she possibly tell the story of her trip from Africa? After all, she was in this English Language Learners classroom along with all of the other students to learn a new language. Until that happened Aminata felt she couldn't possibly tell anyone else what she needed to say. She shook her head and Ms. Simpson asked a boy to go up in her place.

Reread and use the prompts to take notes in the text.

In paragraph 1, draw a box around how the author helps you know what *moi* means. Then underline Aminata's interior monologue.

COLLABORATE

Reread paragraph 2. Circle words and phrases that help you visualize how Aminata feels. Write them here:

_____

_____

1   Aminata nearly cried when she acted out the reunion with her father at the airport in the United States. Her classmates nodded as if they understood exactly how she had felt when she first arrived there.

2   When she finished, Aminata spoke in all the languages she knew: *"Abaraka bake. Merci Beaucoup. Thank you very much."* And then she told everyone something from her heart, in the language of her people, *"Dankutoo le be n' teemaa,"* Aminata said, telling them that they have a bond between them. Aminata held her hands together in front of her chest and smiled, and everyone in the class understood. They nodded back. Aminata added, in halting English, *It is so good to be friends.*

Circle words in paragraph 1 that help you understand how Aminata feels as she tells her story. Draw a box around how her classmates responded.

COLLABORATE

Reread paragraph 2. Underline how the author helps you understand what Aminata is saying. Talk about how you know how she feels. Make marks in the margin beside text evidence that helps you visualize how Aminata and her classmates were feeling. Write it here:

_____

_____

? **What does the author want you to understand about Aminata when she uses French words in class?**

COLLABORATE

Talk About It Reread the excerpt on page 125. Talk with a partner about how the way Aminata tells her story affects her classmates.

Cite Text Evidence What words and phrases tell about Aminata and how she uses her French language? Write text evidence in the chart and tell what it helps you know.

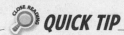
QUICK TIP
When I reread, I can use what the characters say to help me understand how they feel.

Text Evidence	What It Tells

Write The author helps me understand that when Aminata uses her French words it means _____

_____

COLLABORATE

? How are the authors' portrayals of the main characters in *Home of the Brave* and "Aminata's Tale" similar to the way the people are portrayed in the illustration?

Talk About It Look at the illustration. With a partner, discuss what you see. Choose a few images and talk about the differences and similarities you see among the people in the illustration.

Cite Text Evidence Circle three clues in the illustration that help show commonality among the diversity. Draw a box around one example of how people share what they have in common.

Write The portrayal of the people in the illustration is like _____

_____

_____

_____

Ingram Publishing

This wood engraving of a parade on the opening day of the International Exhibition of Arts, Manufactures and Products of the Soil and Mine was created in 1876. It took place on Market Street in Philadelphia, PA.

"This Is Just to Say," "to Mrs. Garcia, in the office," "to Thomas"

 How do the poets use voice to help you see how the poems are different?

Literature Anthology: pages 326–328

Talk About It Reread pages 326–327. Talk with a partner about voice and how it affects the way each poem makes you feel.

Cite Text Evidence What words and phrases help you understand each poem's voice? Write text evidence and tell how the poems are different.

Page 326	Page 327	How They Are Different

Write The poets use voice to show how their poems are different by _____

_____

Tip of the Week

When I **reread**, I can use the poet's words and phrases to understand voice. I look for text evidence to answer questions.

Alfredo

? How does the poet's choice of words help you understand Mrs. Garcia's point of view?

Talk About It Reread page 328. Talk with a partner about how Mrs. Garcia responds to what Thomas has done.

Cite Text Evidence What clues in the poem show how Mrs. Garcia feels? Write text evidence in the chart.

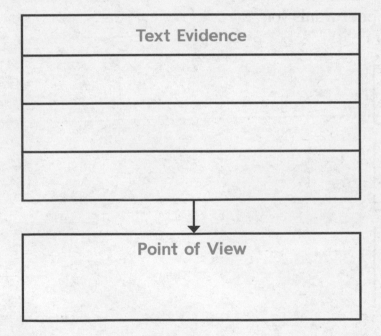

Text Evidence

↓

Point of View

Write The poet helps me understand Mrs. Garcia's point of view by _____

_____

_____

 QUICK TIP

I can use these sentence frames when we talk about point of view.

The poet uses words to show that Mrs. Garcia feels . . .

This helps me see that . . .

Your Turn

How do the poets use voice to help you understand the themes of their poems? Cite evidence from the text using these sentence frames.

Each poet creates a mood by . . .

The poets use voice to show . . .

This helps me understand the theme of the poems by . . .

Go Digital!
Write your response online.

Primer Lesson

? **How does Carl Sandburg's use of sensory language help you understand his poem's message?**

Talk About It Reread page 330. Talk with a partner about what the poet says about proud words.

Cite Text Evidence What words and phrases tell what the poet wants you to know about using proud words? Write text evidence.

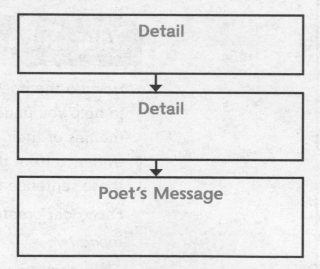

Detail

↓

Detail

↓

Poet's Message

Write Carl Sandburg's use of sensory language helps me understand that _____

_____

_____

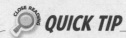 QUICK TIP

When I reread, I can use the author's sensory language to help me understand what his message is.

If I can stop one Heart from Breaking

? How does the way Emily Dickinson organizes her poem create a mood or tone?

COLLABORATE

Talk About It Reread page 331. Talk with a partner about how the poem makes you feel.

Cite Text Evidence What words and phrases does Emily Dickinson use to create mood? Write text evidence in the chart.

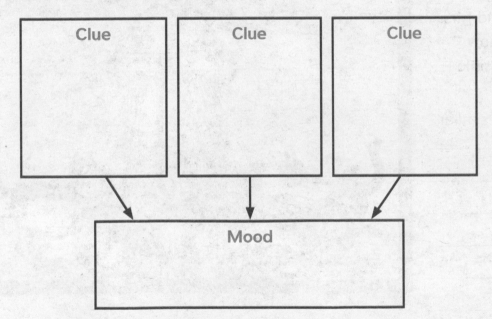

Clue	Clue	Clue

Mood

Write Emily Dickinson organizes her poem to create mood by _____

_____

_____

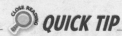

? How is the way the illustrator shows the theme of taking responsibility similar to the way the poets write about taking responsibility in the poems you read this week?

COLLABORATE

Talk About It Look at the illustration. Talk with a partner about what the girl is doing. Discuss what that reveals about the girl's character.

Cite Text Evidence Circle clues that help you understand how the girl in the illustration is taking responsibility and meeting an obligation. Think about how Thomas and Mrs. Garcia feel about taking responsibility. Talk about how words and actions show how people can be responsible for how they treat others.

Write The illustrator shows a form of responsibility similar to the poems because _____

_____

_____

_____

_____

Catherine Lane/iStock/Getty Images Plus/Getty Images

The Hero and the Minotaur: The Fantastic Adventures of Theseus

Literature Anthology: pages 332–347

? How does the author help you understand Poseidon's character and his role in the myth?

COLLABORATE

Talk About It Reread pages 332–333 and analyze the illustration. Talk with a partner about what Poseidon is like.

Cite Text Evidence What words and phrases help you learn what Poseidon is like? Write text evidence and tell what you visualize.

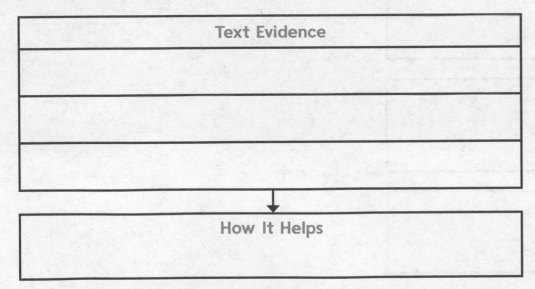

Text Evidence

↓

How It Helps

Write The author helps me understand Poseidon by _____

_____

CLOSE READING

Tip of the Week

When I **reread**, I use the author's words and phrases to help me understand the characters. I look for text evidence to answer questions.

Erin

Darrin Klimek/Photodisc/Getty Images

How does the author help you visualize Theseus' journey to Athens?

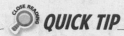 **QUICK TIP**

I can use these sentence frames when we talk about Theseus' journey.

The author uses words and phrases to describe . . .

This helps me visualize . . .

COLLABORATE

Talk About It Reread the last two paragraphs of page 336 and the first paragraph of page 337. Talk with a partner about Theseus' journey.

Cite Text Evidence What phrases describe Theseus' journey to Athens? Write text evidence in the chart.

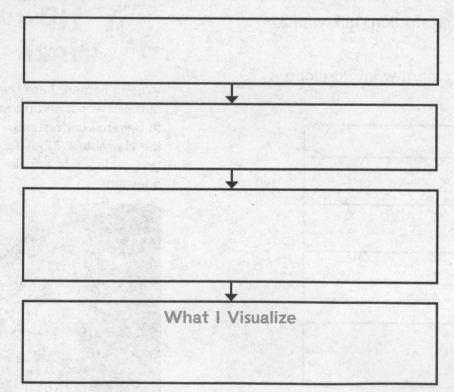

What I Visualize

Write I can visualize Theseus' journey because the author _____

_____

_____

? Why does the author use an idiom to help you visualize how Daedalus feels?

COLLABORATE

Talk About It Reread the second paragraph on page 344. Talk with a partner about how Daedalus feels when Icarus drowned.

Cite Text Evidence What was the author's purpose in using an idiom to describe how Daedalus feels? Write text evidence in the chart.

Text Evidence	Author's Purpose

Write The author uses an idiom to help me visualize how Daedalus feels

because _____

_____

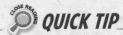 **QUICK TIP**

When I reread, I can use figurative language, like idioms, to help me understand how a character feels.

Your Turn

How does the way the author begins and ends the myth help you understand Poseidon's influence in Theseus' life? Use these sentence frames to organize your text evidence.

The author introduces Poseidon as . . .

The hero takes a voyage to . . .

In the end, Poseidon . . .

Go Digital!
Write your response online.

The A-MAZE-ing Tale of Theseus and the Minotaur

Reread and use the prompts to take notes in the text.

Circle words and phrases that help you understand Theseus' character. Write what Theseus is like.

The Quest Begins

1.   "Look, Theseus! Why don't you try to push this immense rock?" his mother asked, knowing that this was the rock where the king had concealed the sandals and sword.

2.   Even though Theseus thought it was a weird request, and that it was really much too hot to engage in this kind of physical exertion, he did what his mother asked. When he tried to push the rock, however, it wouldn't budge. Growing impatient, Aethra told him to try again, but Theseus still couldn't move the enormous stone.

_____

_____

COLLABORATE

Talk with a partner about your annotations and response above. Discuss how this characterization of Theseus makes the story funny.

_____

_____

3   "Oh, for goodness sake!" Aethra said. Then she leaned on the rock. When she did it went flying down the path and Theseus saw the sword and the sandals.

4   "Cool! Fancy sandals!" Theseus exclaimed and began to slip them on, even though the sandals were a bit crushed after lying out of sight under a rock for 14 years.

5   "Look, Theseus, there's a sword, too," his mother pointed out. Theseus told her she should take it, adding that she could use it to chop lettuce and tomatoes. But Aethra insisted that Theseus would need it more than she would and told him that now he could visit his father, the king.

Circle phrases the author uses to make the story sound like it takes place today instead of thousands of years ago.

COLLABORATE

Underline the sentence that creates suspense. Talk with a partner about how the author makes you want to keep reading.

? How does the author use humor to help you visualize Theseus' character?

COLLABORATE

Talk About It Reread the excerpts on pages 136–137. Talk with a partner about how the parody is funny.

Cite Text Evidence What makes the parody funny? Write text evidence and how it helps you visualize what Theseus is like.

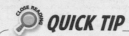
Text Evidence	What I Visualize

Write The author uses humor in this parody to _____

_____

QUICK TIP

I can use illustrations to help me understand how characters feel. This will help me compare art to text.

? How do the artist and authors help you understand how the characters feel in the illustration, *The Hero and the Minotaur*, and "The A-MAZE-ing Tale of Theseus and the Minotaur"?

COLLABORATE

Talk About It Look at the illustration. Talk with a partner about what you see happening and how Icarus feels. Discuss how you know.

Cite Text Evidence What clues in the illustration help you understand how Icarus feels? Work with a partner to circle how the artist shows emotion and action in the characters. Then make a mark beside the illustration that shows Icarus is in danger.

Write The way the artist shows how the characters feel is similar to _____

_____

_____

_____

 (Dorling Kindersley/Getty Images)

This illustration depicts the fall of Icarus after ignoring his father's advice and flying too close to the Sun.

Elijah of Buxton

? How does the author help you visualize how Elijah feels?

Literature Anthology: pages 354–369

COLLABORATE

Talk About It Reread the first paragraph on page 357. Talk with a partner about what is happening to Elijah and how he feels.

Cite Text Evidence How does the author help you visualize how Elijah feels? Write text evidence in the chart and tell what you visualize.

Text Evidence	What I Visualize

Write The author helps me visualize how Elijah feels by _____

_____

_____

Tip of the Week
CLOSE READING

When I **reread**, I use the author's words and phrases to understand how characters feel. I look for text evidence to answer questions.

Manuel

? How does the author use dialogue to help you understand the relationship between Ma and Elijah?

COLLABORATE

Talk About It Reread the first five paragraphs on page 362. Talk about how Elijah feels about what Ma says.

Cite Text Evidence How does the dialogue help you understand what Ma and Elijah are thinking? Write text evidence in the chart.

Ma Says	Elijah Says	What I Understand

Write The author helps me see the relationship between Ma and Elijah

by _____

_____

_____

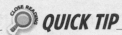
QUICK TIP

I can use these sentence frames when we talk about Elijah and Ma.

Elijah's mother said . . .

The dialogue helps me understand . . .

How does the author show that Elijah's character is growing?

Talk About It Reread the last six paragraphs of the story on page 368. Talk with a partner about Elijah's point of view about the women.

Cite Text Evidence What descriptive language does the author use to show how Elijah sees and experiences the women's support? Write text evidence in the chart.

Text Evidence

↓

How I Know

Write I know Elijah is growing because the author _____

_____

_____

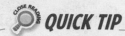 **QUICK TIP**

When I reread, I think about the author's words and phrases to help me understand how characters feel.

Your Turn

Think about Elijah's transformation from boyhood to adolescence. How does the author show Elijah's inner strength on his journey to adulthood? Use these sentence frames to organize your text evidence.

The author describes how Elijah feels by . . .

He uses dialogue to . . .

This helps show that Elijah . . .

Go Digital!
Write your response online.

The People Could Fly

How does the illustration help you understand how the people in the folktale felt?

COLLABORATE

Talk About It Look at the illustration on page 372. Talk with a partner about how the people look and what they are doing.

Cite Text Evidence What details in the illustration help you understand how flying made the people feel? Write them in the chart.

Illustration	What It Means

Write The illustration helps me understand that the people in the folktale

_____

_____

QUICK TIP
When I reread, I can use the illustrations to help me understand how characters feel.

How does the author help you understand what working was like for the slaves?

COLLABORATE

Talk About It Reread the sixth paragraph on page 373. Talk with a partner about what kind of person the Master was.

Cite Text Evidence What phrases describe the way the Master treats the slaves? Write text evidence.

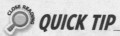
QUICK TIP
When I reread, I can use the author's words and phrases to help me understand events in a folktale.

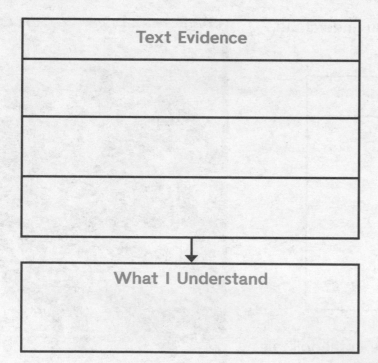

Text Evidence

↓

What I Understand

Write I understand what it was like to work as a slave because the author

_____

_____

How does the author help you visualize Sarah's flight?

Talk About It Reread the third and fourth paragraphs on page 374. Talk with a partner about how Sarah flies.

Cite Text Evidence How does the author describe how Sarah takes flight? Write text evidence in the chart.

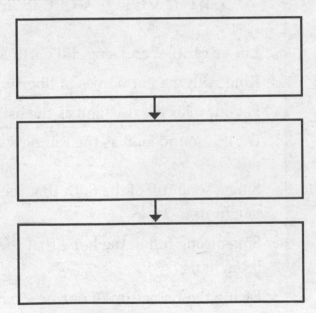

Write The author helps me visualize Sarah's flight by _____

_____

_____

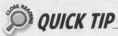 **QUICK TIP**

I can use these sentence frames to help me visualize Sarah's flight.

The author describes what happened by . . .

This helps me visualize . . .

? How do the song lyrics and sensory language in *Elijah of Buxton* and "The People Could Fly" help you visualize the characters' inner strength?

COLLABORATE

Talk About It Read the lyrics. Talk with a partner about how James Weldon Johnson shares how he feels.

Cite Text Evidence Underline words and phrases that work together to convey the theme of inner strength. Circle text evidence to support how the author feels.

Write The song lyrics and stories I read this week help me visualize _____

_____

_____

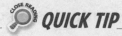

QUICK TIP

I can use sensory language in lyrics to help me visualize. Then I can compare it to the stories I read this week.

Lift Every Voice and Sing

Lift ev'ry voice and sing, till earth and heaven ring,

Ring with the harmonies of liberty.

Let our rejoicing rise high as the list'ning skies,

Let it resound loud as the rolling sea.

Sing a song full of the faith that the dark past has taught us;

Sing a song full of the hope that the present has brought us;

Facing the rising sun of our new day begun,

Let us march on till victory is won.

— James Weldon Johnson

Design Pics/Ken Welsh

Published just thirty-five years after the official end of slavery, this African American song celebrates freedom.

Before Columbus: The Americas of 1491

Literature Anthology: pages 376–387

? How does the author use illustrations to help you understand more about maize?

COLLABORATE

Talk About It Look at the image on page 378. Talk with a partner about what it shows and how it helps you understand the selection.

Cite Text Evidence What details in the image tell you more about maize? Write clues in the chart and tell how they help.

Clues	How They Help

Write The author uses illustrations to _____

_____

CLOSE READING
Tip of the Week

When I **reread**, I can use photographs to help me understand more about the topic.

Roshan

What is the author's point of view about the invention of the *milpa*?

Talk About It Reread the first two paragraphs on page 384. Talk with a partner about what the *milpa* is.

Cite Text Evidence What text evidence shows how the author feels about the invention of the *milpa*? Write it in the chart.

Text Evidence
Text Evidence
Text Evidence
Author's Point of View

Write The author's point of view about the invention of the *milpa* is _____

_____

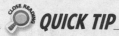 **QUICK TIP**

I can use these sentence frames when we talk about the *milpa*.

The author describes the milpa as . . .

His point of view is . . .

? How does the author use the map to help you understand maize and its impact on Mesoamerica?

COLLABORATE

Talk About It Reread page 386 and analyze the map on page 387. Talk with a partner about Mesoamerica and how it supports the text.

Cite Text Evidence How does the map help clarify the text? Write text evidence in the chart.

Evidence from the Map	How It Clarifies Text

Write The author uses the map to help me understand _____

_____

_____

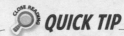

QUICK TIP
When I reread, I can use a map to clarify information in the text.

Your Turn

How does Charles C. Mann use text features and organization of this selection to help you understand how people benefited from the innovation of maize? Use these sentence frames to organize your text evidence.

Charles C. Mann uses illustrations, sidebars, and maps to . . .

He shares his point of view to help me . . .

I see how people benefited from the innovation of maize because . . .

Go Digital!
Write your response online.

Looking Back to Move Forward

Ancient Cures

1   Over two decades ago, two divers plunged into the murky depths of the Mediterranean Sea off the coast of Italy. Their mission was the exploration of a 50-foot long shipwreck. It had been lost beneath the waves over 2,000 years ago. As they trained their underwater lights across the vast hulk, they spotted amphorae-vases used for holding olive oil and other products. But a close inspection revealed something much more remarkable. Pulled from the wreck, the explorers found tin-lined wooden containers. They held tablets the size of small coins.

2   Scientists later found that these tablets were probably pills that the ship's sailors would have swallowed with water, perhaps when they felt seasick. This sort of medicine is nothing new to us today. At the time, however, they must have been something new, for they may be the oldest pills discovered.

Reread and use the prompts to take notes in the text.

Circle the sentences from the introduction that tell what the explorers discovered. Star the sentence that tells why this discovery is important.

COLLABORATE

Talk with a partner about the discovery and its importance. How do you think this discovery could affect science today?

_____

_____

_____

[3] Researchers also continue to look at the past in order to investigate cures that were used long ago. One such opportunity presented itself with the discovery of that ancient Roman shipwreck in the Mediterranean. Although the pills were discovered in 1989, recent advances in DNA research are now making it possible to better understand what chemical compounds these pills contained. This research will also help determine what illnesses the pills were used to treat. The hope is that advances in technology will build upon ancient wisdom.

Reread the last paragraph of the text. Underline the sentences that tell how researchers today use such discoveries as the tablets from the shipwreck. Explain in your own words:

_____

_____

_____

COLLABORATE

Talk with a partner about why ancient medicines are of interest to the scientific community. How can we benefit from the knowledge they gain about these substances?

_____

_____

_____

Why is "Looking Back to Move Forward" a good title for this selection?

COLLABORATE

Talk About It Reread the first paragraph on page 150 and the paragraph on page 151. Talk with a partner about your observations.

Cite Text Evidence Record text evidence of each of the excerpted paragraphs. Explain the author's purpose for concluding the passage this way.

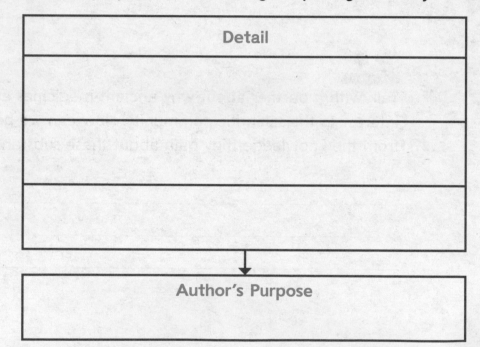

Detail

↓

Author's Purpose

Write The author's purpose _____

_____

_____

_____

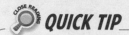
QUICK TIP

When I reread, I consider the author's purpose and the text's organization.

? How is pre-European innovation made apparent by this aerial photograph, the investigation into the origin of maize in *Before Columbus: The Americas of 1491,* and the discovery of medicine in an ancient Roman shipwreck in "Looking Back to Move Forward"?

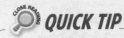

COLLABORATE

Talk About It Look at the photograph and read the caption. Talk with a partner about the location of the buildings, their size, and the technology the Incan civilization must have used to create such an elaborate site.

Cite Text Evidence Circle clues in the photograph that show the advanced engineering that was needed for the construction of Machu Picchu. Underline evidence in the caption that tells when it was built. Think about the selections you read this week. Talk about how important innovation is and how people benefit from it.

Write I understand how important innovation is

because _____

_____

_____

_____

Glow Images

QUICK TIP

I see challenges to innovation in the photograph. This helps me compare art to text.

This photograph presents an aerial view of the Machu Picchu site in the Cusco Region of Peru. This grand group of structures was built before the Spanish Conquest in the mid-1400s by the Incan civilization.

Planet Hunter

? Why is the photograph essential to understanding the author's description of Mauna Kea?

Talk About It Reread page 395. Talk with a partner about why the photograph is important.

Cite Text Evidence What clues from the text and photograph help you understand what Mauna Kea is like? Write text evidence in the chart.

Text Evidence	Photograph Clues	What I Know

Write The photograph is essential to understanding the author's description of

Mauna Kea because _____

_____

Literature Anthology: pages 394–407

Tip of the Week

When I **reread**, I can think about how the author uses words and phrases. I look for text evidence to answer questions.

Inez

Daniel Bendjy/E-plus/Getty Images

How do you know how Marcy feels about his work?

Talk About It Reread the last two paragraphs on page 400. Talk with a partner about what Marcy says about his research.

Cite Text Evidence How does the author help you understand Marcy's passion for the work he does? Write text evidence in the chart.

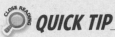 **QUICK TIP**

I can use these sentence frames when we talk about Marcy's work.

The author uses quotes to tell me that Marcy . . .

This helps me know that he . . .

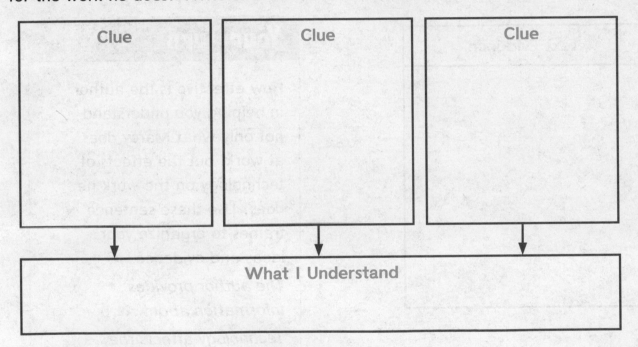

Clue	Clue	Clue

What I Understand

Write I know how Marcy feels about his work because the author _____

_____

How does the way the author organizes the text help you understand what Marcy does at work?

 **QUICK TIP**

I can analyze the way the author organizes text to help me understand the topic.

Talk About It Reread page 406. Talk with a partner about what you notice about the way each paragraph is written.

Cite Text Evidence What two ways does the author show what Marcy does at work? Write text evidence in the chart.

What the Author Does	Text Evidence

Write The author organizes the text by _____

_____

_____

Your Turn

How effective is the author in helping you understand not only what Marcy does at work, but the effects of technology on the work he does? Use these sentence frames to organize your ideas and evidence.

The author provides information about . . .

Technology affects the team's work by . . .

The author clarifies details about the technology by . . .

Go Digital!
Write your response online.

Excursion to Mars

News from PERC

1   The eighth grade advanced teleportation class was working on some calculations when a hologram suddenly appeared in the front of the room. Everyone stopped talking and turned to look because the last time a hologram appeared in class it had bad news about a space disaster. Keisha bit her lip as she waited for the news.

2   "Congratulations, Keisha and Gene!" it said." You have won the Planet Earth Robotics Competition for the year 2172!"

Reread and use the prompts to take notes in the text.

Make notes in the margins about how Keisha and Gene are like people today. Circle details that tell how their lives are different.

Talk with a partner about how you know how Keisha feels. Underline text evidence and write it here:

_____

_____

3   The class erupted in applause, and Keisha ran to hug the woman in the hologram that had made the announcement. Her arms just passed through the 3-D light image.

4   "I can't believe we won!" Keisha exclaimed as the hologram disappeared.

5   "Of course we won," said Gene, with his typical matter-of-fact tone, "and that's because our robot, Anisisbro, has the ability to navigate any environment—on wheels, in the air, or in water—and also because of our original thought coding, so it comes up with creative solutions to problems by itself, and can execute solutions."

Underline the phrase that helps you visualize what a hologram is. Write it here:

_____

Circle text evidence that tells what Gene is like.

COLLABORATE

Talk with a partner about how the author describes Anisisbro. Make marks in the margin beside words and phrases that tell what the robot can do.

? How does the author help you visualize the fictional technology in the story?

COLLABORATE

Talk About It Reread the excerpt on page 158. Talk about the hologram and Anisisbro and how you know what they do.

Cite Text Evidence What words and phrases tell what the hologram and Anisisbro do? Write text evidence in the chart.

Hologram	Anisisbro	What I Visualize

Write The author helps me visualize the fictional technology in the story

by _____

_____

_____

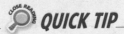
QUICK TIP

When I reread, I can use the author's words and phrases to help me visualize the fictional technology in the story.

Integrate

? How does this etching of a constellation help you understand how technology can lead to discoveries like the ones discussed in *Planet Hunter,* as well as ideas presented in "Excursion to Mars"?

QUICK TIP
I see both science and fiction in this etching. This will help me compare it to the selections I read this week.

Talk About It Look at the illustration. Talk with a partner about what you see in the etching. Discuss how this art connects with what you learned about astronomy in *Planet Hunter.*

Cite Text Evidence Circle clues in the etching that are fictional, or imaginative, like the events in "Excursion to Mars." Underline clues that are based on the science of astronomy.

Write From this 1825 etching of a constellation, I understand _____

_____

_____

_____

This hand-colored etching by Sidney Hall depicts the constellation Boötes, the Ploughman, and the dogs Asterion and Chara.

Library of Congress Prints and Photographs Division [LC-USZC4-I0059]

Out of This World

? How does the graph help you understand the development of the International Space Station?

Literature Anthology:
pages 414–417

COLLABORATE

Talk About It Reread page 415 and analyze the graph. Talk with a partner about technology and the space program.

Cite Text Evidence What evidence from the graph shows the development of the International Space Station? Write text evidence in the chart.

Evidence	What I Understand

Write The author uses a graph to help me see the development of the space

station by _____

_____

Tip of the Week
CLOSE READING

When I **reread**, I can use text features to help me understand complex information. I look for text evidence to answer questions.

Darrell

? How does the time line support the author's message about evolving technology?

COLLABORATE

Talk About It Analyze the time line on page 416. Talk with a partner about how the time line helps you understand the events of space exploration.

Cite Text Evidence What clues in the time line tell about how technology has evolved? Write text evidence in the chart.

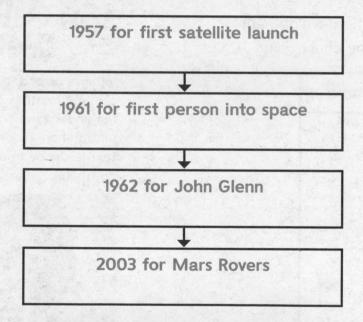

1957 for first satellite launch

↓

1961 for first person into space

↓

1962 for John Glenn

↓

2003 for Mars Rovers

Write I understand the author's message about evolving technology because the time line _____

_____

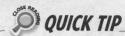

QUICK TIP

When I reread, I can use the time line to understand the sequence of events and how it supports the author's message.

Your Turn

How does the author use text features to help you understand the evolving technology used in the space program? Use these sentence frames to organize your text evidence.

The author uses graphs and a time line to . . .

He shows how technology has evolved by . . .

This helps me understand that . . .

Go Digital!
Write your response online.

Space Shuttles on the Move

Intrepid Sea, Air & Space Museum/AP Images

[1]   When NASA's space shuttle program ended in 2011, a decision had to be made. What should be done with some of the spaceships that had been taking off from Cape Canaveral in Florida since 1981? One newspaper made a few computations about the space shuttle *Discovery*, and made it sound as if NASA were selling a used car: "27 years old, 150 million miles traveled, somewhat damaged but well maintained. Price: $0. Dealer preparation and destination charges: $28.8 million.

[2]   Damaged or not, civic leaders, museum workers, and space buffs in 29 cities around the country eagerly awaited NASA's decision about where *Discovery* would end up. The space shuttles *Endeavor, Atlantis,* and *Enterprise* were also ending their careers in space, and their final destinations also had to be decided.

The retired space shuttles will go on display at various locations around the United States.

Reread and use the prompts to take notes in the text.

Circle the sentence in paragraph 1 that helps you know what NASA officials needed to decide. Write it here:

_____

_____

COLLABORATE

Reread paragraph 2. Talk with a partner about who wanted the retired space shuttles. Underline text evidence.

Look at the illustration and read the caption. Circle clues that show that community leaders are eager to host retired space shuttles.

? How do the illustrations and captions help you better understand what happens to retired space shuttles?

COLLABORATE

Talk About It Look at the illustration on page 163. Talk with a partner about what communities might do with a space shuttle.

Cite Text Evidence What clues in the illustration and caption help show what happens when space shuttles are retired? Write evidence in the chart.

Clues	Author's Purpose

Write The author uses illustrations and captions to help me _____

_____

_____

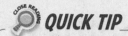

QUICK TIP

When I reread, I can use illustrations and captions to help me understand the topic.

? How does the tone of Emily Dickinson's poem "The Railway Train" compare to the tone presented in "Out of This World" and "Space Shuttles on the Move"?

Talk About It Read the poem "The Railway Train." Talk about the narrator's tone, or attitude toward the train. Keep in mind that when the poem was written, trains were a relatively new form of technology.

Cite Text Evidence Circle five examples where the poet personifies the train. Write in the margins the comparison she makes.

Write The tone of the poem compares to the tone of the selections I read this week because

_____

_____

_____

_____

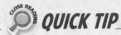

QUICK TIP

I see sensory language in the poem that helps me understand tone. This will help me compare the poem to the selections I read this week.

The Railway Train

I like to see it lap the miles,
And lick the valleys up,
And stop to feed itself at tanks;
And then, prodigious, step

Around a pile of mountains,
And, supercilious, peer
In shanties by the sides of roads;
And then a quarry pare

To fit its sides, and crawl between,
Complaining all the while
In horrid, hooting stanza;
Then chase itself down hill

And neigh like Boanerges;
Then, punctual as a star,
Stop—docile and omnipotent—
At it's own stable door.

— Emily Dickinson

The Story of Salt

? How does the author use the sidebar to help you understand the main text?

COLLABORATE

Talk About It Reread the sidebar on page 422. Talk with a partner about what you learned about salt.

Cite Text Evidence What details help you understand more about salt? Write text evidence in the chart.

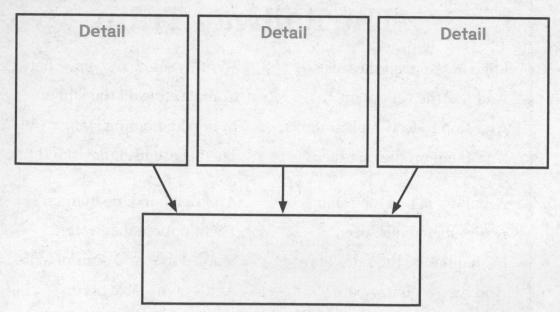

Detail	Detail	Detail

Write The sidebar connects to the main text because _____

_____

_____

Literature Anthology: pages 420–435

CLOSE READING

Tip of the Week

When I **reread**, I can use sidebars to understand complex ideas. I find text evidence to answer questions.

Mateo

Jack Hollingsworth/Photodisc/Getty Images

How does the author make it clear which type of text this is?

Talk About It Reread pages 424 and 425. Talk with a partner about clues that show this text is expository.

Cite Text Evidence How do you know this is an expository text? Write text evidence in the chart.

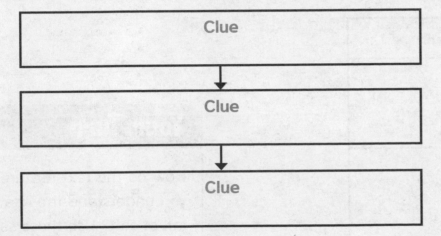

Clue

↓

Clue

↓

Clue

Write The author makes it clear that this is an _____

_____

_____

 QUICK TIP

I can use these sentence frames when we talk about expository text.

The author . . .

This helps me see that . . .

? **How does the author use a timeline to help you understand the selection?**

COLLABORATE

Talk About It Reread the timeline on pages 434 and 435. With a partner, talk about some important ideas in the timeline.

Cite Text Evidence What details support important information you learned from the timeline? Write text evidence in the chart.

What I Learned	Text Evidence

Write The timeline helps me understand the selection by _____

_____

_____

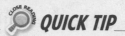 **QUICK TIP**

When I reread, I can use information in a timeline to learn more about a topic.

Your Turn

How do the text features help you understand the rise and fall of salt? Use these sentence frames to organize your text evidence.

The author uses sidebars to . . .

He uses illustrations and time lines to . . .

This helps me understand . . .

Go Digital!
Write your response online.

"The Not-So-Golden Touch"

Peter Malone

[1]   Long ago, a king named Midas ruled a large and peaceful kingdom. Midas loved to look at his paintings and his castle's fine furnishings, but most of all, he loved the large gold goblet and the golden statues that his staff polished every day. Midas knew he was a very lucky man to live surrounded by such beauty, but he also knew that the many golden objects in his possession made him a very rich man. Gold was a very rare and valuable commodity.

[2]   Midas was, however, not a terribly thoughtful man, and he tended to speak first and think later. One day Midas was riding in his carriage when he saw an old man sound aslep under a tree on the palace grounds. Midas was about to request that the trespasser be told to get off his property when one of Midas's minions woke up saying, "Surely we can let his sleep here your highness. He is an old man after all."

[3]   King Midas thought about it and agreed saying "Yes, let him sleep."

Reread and use the prompts to take notes in the text.

Circle the words that reveal King Midas's status.

Place a star next to the example of King Midas speaking first and thinking later.

COLLABORATE

With a partner, underline the sentence that lets readers know the importance of gold as a resource. Talk about two different reasons that Midas loved gold. Write them here:

_____

_____

1. With that issue resolved, the king went to sleep happy, and the next morning he ordered a special breakfast. When it arrived, he picked up a silver fork, which immediately turned to gold. Then he took a bite of the steak and, following that, ate a forkful of egg, but somehow he felt disappointed. Something was missing, for this food didn't taste nearly as delicious as he remembered, and so the king immediately called for the cook.

2. Between Midas's outbursts, the cook tried patiently to explain that there was in fact something missing. Salt! Salt was now too valuable for anyone-even a king- to use as a seasoning on food.

3. The king sighed and picked at his bland food. He was beginning to realize what events he had set in motion and how, because of his greed, his food would never taste the same again.

Reread the excerpt from the story. Circle details that tell you the king thinks he has solved all of his problems. Write the two problems the king still has here:

1. _____

2. _____

COLLABORATE

Talk with a partner about why it's a problem that they have chosen to replace gold with salt as currency. Underline why the king can no longer put salt on his food.

Peter Malone

? How does the author show the importance of thinking ahead?

COLLABORATE

Talk About It Look back at page 169 and 170. Talk with a partner about Midas's mistake in the story.

Cite Text Evidence How does the author foreshadow King Midas's mistake? Write text evidence in the chart.

Action	Consequence

Write The author shows thinking ahead is important by _____

_____

_____

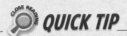
QUICK TIP

When I reread, I can use words and phrases to help me understand the author's message.

 **QUICK TIP**

The illustration shows what was important to people in the past. This helps me compare text to art.

? How does the illustrator use details to help you understand the importance of natural resources similar to the way the authors of *The Story of Salt* and "The Not-So-Golden Touch" use text features?

Talk About It Look at the illustration. Describe to a partner what you see and how you know what the people are doing is important.

Cite Text Evidence Circle clues in the illustration that show what is being transported. Then underline how you know this is an important part of life for these people. Think about how important salt is.

Write The details in the illustration and text features in the selections help me to

_____

_____

_____

_____

Peter Dennis/Getty Images

This illustration of a 13th century camel caravan shows Marco Polo's merchants, camels, and horses.

The Great Fire

? How does the author use cause and effect relationships to help you understand why it was so difficult to extinguish the fire?

Literature Anthology:
pages 442–457

COLLABORATE

Talk About It Reread the third paragraph on page 448. Talk with a partner about why the fire continued to burn.

Cite Text Evidence What details help you understand what happened and why the fire was so difficult to extinguish? Write text evidence in the chart.

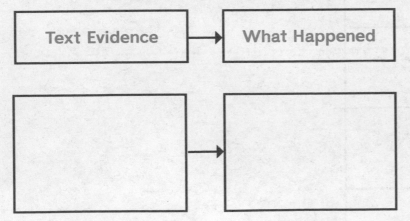

Text Evidence	→	What Happened
	→	

Write The author uses cause and effect to help me understand _____

_____

Tip of the Week

CLOSE READING

When I **reread**, I can use signal words and phrases. I look for text evidence to answer questions.

Gabrielle

Radius Images/Alamy

? **How does the author help you understand the fire's devastation?**

Talk About It Reread the first full paragraph on page 451. Talk with a partner about how Alfred Sewell describes how people felt.

Cite Text Evidence What words and phrases help you visualize the devastation caused by the fire and how people felt? Write text evidence in the chart.

Text Evidence
Text Evidence
Text Evidence
What I Understand

Write The author includes this description to _____

_____

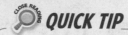 **QUICK TIP**

I can use these sentence frames when we talk about primary sources.

The quote reveals . . .

Reading a first person account helps me understand . . .

? **What was the author's purpose for including why Julia Lemos left her house?**

Talk About It Reread the two paragraphs on page 456. With a partner, talk about what caused Julia Lemos to leave.

Cite Text Evidence How does the author show Julia Lemos' determination to keep her family safe?

Text Evidence	Author's Purpose

Write The author included these details to show _____
_____

QUICK TIP
When I reread, I notice how the author uses cause and effect relationships.

Your Turn

How does Jim Murphy's use of cause and effect help you understand the story of the great Chicago fire? Use these sentence frames to organize your text evidence.

Jim Murphy uses words and phrase to describe . . .

He organizes the text to show causes and effects to . . .

This helps me understand . . .

Go Digital!
Write your response online.

Aftermath of a Fire

? How does Frederick Law Olmstead use cause and effect to convey tone?

Talk About It Reread Frederick Law Olmstead's article on page 461. Talk with a partner about what Olmstead thinks about the Chicago Fire.

Cite Text Evidence What words and phrases show how the inferior building materials contributed to the fire? Write text evidence in the graphic organizer.

Text Evidence	Author's Point of View

Write The author uses cause and effect to _____

_____

_____

? How do the introduction and caption make Frederick Law Olmstead's article credible, or believable?

Talk About It Reread the introduction and caption on page 461. Talk with a partner about how the caption supports what Olmstead thinks.

Cite Text Evidence What clues show that Olmstead's point of view can be trusted? Write text evidence in the chart and explain how.

Text Evidence	Why I Can Trust Him

Write The introduction and caption help support Olmstead's article by _____

_____

_____

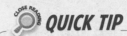

? What is Olmstead suggesting about the devastation of the Chicago Fire?

Talk About It Turn and talk with a partner about the tone you can determine from Olmsted's article. What is his opinion about the fire?

Cite Text Evidence What clues help you understand how Olmstead feels about the Chicago Fire? Write text evidence and explain his perspective in the chart.

Clue	Author's Perspective

Write Olmsted's tone suggests that _____

_____

_____

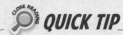

QUICK TIP
When I reread, I notice how the author feels about a subject and how he is trying to make me feel.

? In what ways is the mood of the photograph similar to the first hand accounts in *The Great Fire* and "Aftermath of a Fire"?

COLLABORATE

Talk About It Look at the photograph and read the caption. Talk with a partner about how the woman and her family live. Discuss how the photograph makes you feel.

Cite Text Evidence Circle clues in the photograph that show how hard life is for the family. Underline text evidence in the caption that gives you more information about how this real family lived. Compare what you learn from this historical photograph with what the first hand accounts help you understand about the Great Fire.

Write The photographer and the authors use real historical photographs and accounts to _____

_____

_____

USDA Photograph Archives

QUICK TIP

This photograph accurately depicts how life was for one family during the Great Depression. It will help me compare how historical evidence is important in the selections I read this week.

This photograph by Dorothea Lange was taken during the Great Depression in November, 1940. The family came from Amarillo, Texas and worked their way through New Mexico and Arizona by picking cotton. They lived in a trailer in an open field with no water.

Extreme Scientists

? What effect do the details about Hazel's early life have on how you feel about her?

Talk About It Reread the last paragraph on page 465. Talk to a partner about what the paragraph tells you about Hazel's early life.

Cite Text Evidence What details about Hazel's early life help you understand more about her? Write text evidence in the chart.

Text Evidence	Effect

Write The details about Hazel's early life help me understand that _____

_____

Literature Anthology: pages 462–477

When I **reread**, I look for details in the biography that help me learn more about someone.

Sarah

? How does the author use captions to help you understand more about what Hazel does?

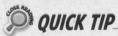

QUICK TIP

I can use these sentence frames when we talk about Hazel's job.

New information I learned from the captions is . . .

This helps me understand . . .

Talk About It Reread the captions on pages 468 and 469. Talk with a partner about what you learned about Hazel's job and microbes.

Cite Text Evidence Compare and contrast the information in the text with the information in the captions. Write text evidence in the diagram

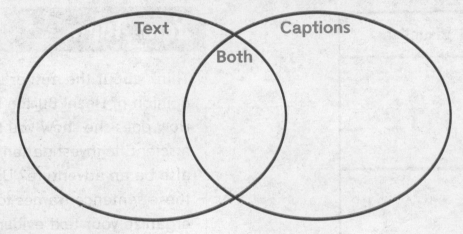

Text   Captions

Both

Write The author includes the information in the photo captions because _____

_____

_____

? How does the author's use of descriptive language help you visualize what it was like to get to the testing site?

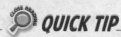

QUICK TIP

When I reread, I understand that every word the author uses is a deliberate choice.

COLLABORATE

Talk About It Reread the third paragraph on page 472. Talk with a partner about how the author describes the journey to the site.

Cite Text Evidence What words and phrases help you visualize how the cavers got to the testing site? Write text evidence in the chart.

Text Evidence	What I Visualize

Write The author uses descriptive language to help me visualize _____

_____

_____

Your Turn

Think about the author's opinion of Hazel Burton's job. How does she show you that a scientific investigation can also be an adventure? Use these sentence frames to organize your text evidence.

The author uses photographs and captions to help me understand . . .

Her words describe how Hazel Burton . . .

This is important because it helps me . . .

Go Digital!
Write your response online.

"Making the Scientific Method Work For You"

1   Usually, right-handed batters hit better against left-handed pitchers and vice-versa. So if a right-handed pitcher is playing on the opposing team, Marta's coach sometimes sends her onto the field to bat left-handed.

2   Still, Marta writes with her right hand, so her right hand is said to be her "dominant hand." She has also noticed that she hits more home runs when she bats right-handed. Based on further observation and a number of trials, she developed the following hypothesis: "While I get hits batting left or right-handed, if I bat with my dominant hand all the time then I will get more hits."

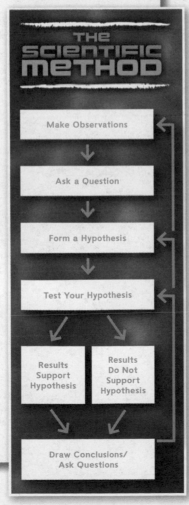

THE SCIENTIFIC METHOD

Make Observations

Ask a Question

Form a Hypothesis

Test Your Hypothesis

Results Support Hypothesis

Results Do Not Support Hypothesis

Draw Conclusions/ Ask Questions

Reread and use the prompts to take notes in the text.

Underline the observations Marta makes before developing a hypothesis.

COLLABORATE

Reread paragraph 2. With a partner circle the hypothesis. Talk about how Marta came up with her hypothesis.

_____

_____

Reread the sidebar. Number the steps of the scientific method. Circle the decision that has to be made to test a hypothesis. How does the sidebar help you understand the scientific method?

3   In a scientific experiment, *Control* means a factor which always remains the same. A *Variable* is something that can vary according to the situation. When you have finished recording your scores in the "Control" column, you need to test the subject's reaction time with his or her non-dominant hand. This is the variable. Then switch places. The subject becomes the tester, and the tester becomes the subject. Compare reaction times in both control groups with those in the variable groups.

How does the author help you understand what *control* and *variable* are? Underline text evidence in paragraph 1.

COLLABORATE

Talk with a partner about how the author uses examples to explain *control* and *variable*. Circle the text where the author uses an example to help readers understand the term *variable*.

? What is the author's purpose for writing "Making the Scientific Method Work For You"?

Talk About It Reread the excerpt on page 184. Talk to a partner about why the author wrote this selection.

Cite Text Evidence What clues help you figure out the author's purpose? Write text evidence in the chart.

Clues	Author's Purpose

Write The author wrote "Making the Scientific Method Work For You?"

because _____

_____

? How do Walt Whitman's feelings about the scientific method compare to how Hazel Barton feels about what she does in *Extreme Scientists*?

COLLABORATE

Talk About It Read the poem. Talk with a partner about what the narrator is describing and how he feels about figures and columns and charts. Discuss what the narrator does at the end of the poem.

Cite Text Evidence Circle words that show how the narrator feels in the lecture room. Underline clues that help you understand how he feels when he is outdoors. Think about how Hazel Barton feels about her job.

Write I see how the narrator and Hazel Barton's point of views compare because _____

_____

_____

_____

_____

QUICK TIP

Walt Whitman's words help me understand his point of view. This helps me compare the poem to text.

When I Heard the Learn'd Astronomer

When I heard the learn'd astronomer,

When the proofs, the figures, were ranged in columns before me,

When I was shown the charts and diagrams, to add, divide, and measure them,

When I sitting heard the astronomer where he lectured with much applause in the lecture-room,

How soon unaccountable I became tired and sick,

Till rising and gliding out I wander'd off by myself,

In the mystical moist night-air, and from time to time,

Look'd up in perfect silence at the stars.

— Walt Whitman

Pharaoh's Boat

Literature Anthology:
pages 484–499

? **How does the author use a list to support the text?**

Talk About It Reread page 489 and look at the list. Talk with a partner about why the author includes illustrations.

Cite Text Evidence What details help you understand some of the reasons for the tools? Write them in the web.

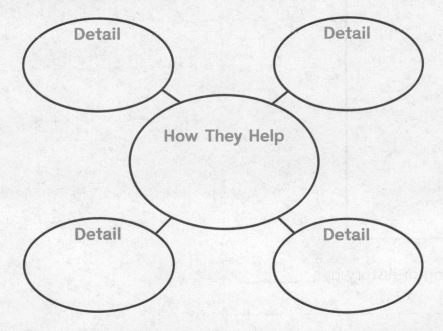

- Detail
- Detail
- How They Help
- Detail
- Detail

Tip of the Week

When I **reread**, I can use text features to help me understand more about the topic.

Amanda

Write The author uses the list to help me understand _____

_____

_____

Jupiterimages/Stockbyte/Getty Images

? How does the author help you understand Mallakh's feeling of history?

Talk About It Reread the second paragraph on page 493. Discuss with a partner the sensory language Mallakh uses.

Cite Text Evidence What clues help Mallakh draw a conclusion? Write text evidence and your conclusion in the chart.

Clues	Conclusion

Write The author helps me understand Mallakh's feeling of history by _____

_____

_____

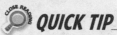 **QUICK TIP**

I can use these sentence frames when we talk about sensory language.

When the author says . . .

I can visualize . . .

? How does the author help you understand Ahmed's struggle to rebuild the ancient ship?

Talk About It Reread the first paragraph on page 496. Talk with a partner about why it's difficult to build an ancient ship.

Cite Text Evidence What problems does Ahmed face and how is he able to solve the problems? Write text evidence in the chart.

Problem	Solution

Write The author helps me understand Ahmad's struggle by _____

_____

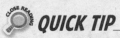

QUICK TIP
When I reread, I make sure I notice problems in the text and how they are solved.

Your Turn

Why does the author include the history of pharaohs and their importance on Egyptian culture? Use these sentence frames to organize your text evidence.

The illustrations and captions help me to ...

The author also uses historical details to ...

This helps me understand ...

Go Digital!
Write your response online.

"The Mystery of the Missing Sandals"

Reread and use the prompts to take notes in the text.

Underline facts in the excerpt that can be verified in the mystery.

COLLABORATE

How does the text's point of view reveal that it comes from a piece of fiction? Talk with a partner about what details in the paragraph were made up. Write them here:

_____

_____

1   Starting in June, the museum had started getting pretty crowded because it had a traveling exhibit on King Tutankhamun. That's King Tut to you. The exhibit is filled with incredible artifacts, even an alabaster jar with a sculpture of the king on top that once held King Tut's mummified stomach. In case you don't know, Tut was sort of a minor king, but the ancient Egyptians still buried him in style in a tomb archaeologist Howard Carter unearthed in 1922.

Read paragraph 1. Underline a sentence that reflects a scientist's technique of questioning.

COLLABORATE

How does the author address the question? Talk with a partner about the different conclusions that Alice shares with Scott.

1   "Oh, hi Scott," Alice answered as she looked up. "It's one of several boats in the collection from King Tut's tomb, and I'm just giving it a final inspection for the exhibit. This is the smallest one. And I've uncovered this amazing detail—see this extra hole on the deck? I'm guessing there might have been another mast on this boat that was broken off long ago."

2   "Why were there so many boats found in the tomb?" I wondered aloud. "Wasn't Tutankhamun buried in the desert?"

3   "Boats were extremely important to the Egyptians," Alice answered. "The Nile River was their lifeblood."

Why does the author use factual details in this fictional mystery?

COLLABORATE

Talk About It Reread the excerpt on page 190. Talk with a partner about how the facts add to the mystery.

Cite Text Evidence What examples of factual and fictional details did the author include? Write them in the chart.

Fact	Fiction

Write The author uses factual details in a fictional mystery because _____

_____

_____

? How does the photographer's task of documenting this mummy compare with the way the author tells about the boat in *Pharoah's Boat* to help you understand the importance of artifacts?

webking/iStock/Getty Images Plus/Getty Images

COLLABORATE

Talk About It Look at the photograph and read the caption. Talk with a partner about what you see. Discuss the value of having photographs of artifacts.

Cite Text Evidence Circle details in the photograph that tell about the ancient civilization this mummy was part of when he was alive. Think about how this artifact and the remains of the Pharoah's boat help scientists learn about other people and how they lived.

Write The photographer's task is like the author's because

_____

_____

_____

_____

QUICK TIP

I see details in the photograph that help me to understand how the person lived. This will help me compare the photograph to text.

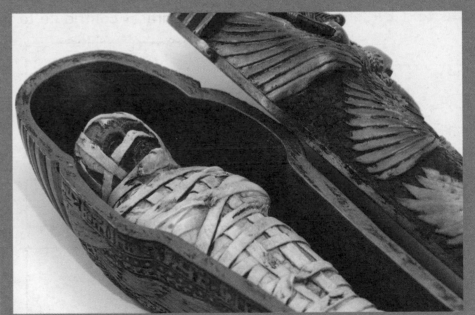

This mummy was discovered and photographed so that scientists and archaeologists could learn about how the young man lived.

"To You,"
"Ode to Pablo's Tennis Shoes"

Literature Anthology:
pages 506–509

? How does the imagery in the poem connect to the poem's theme?

COLLABORATE

Talk About It Reread page 507. Turn and talk with a partner about the examples of imagery in the poem.

Cite Text Evidence What words and phrases contribute to the poem's theme?

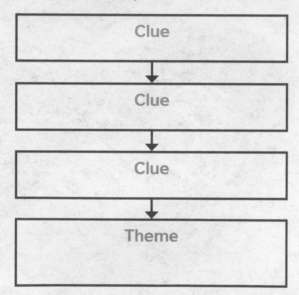

Clue
↓
Clue
↓
Clue
↓
Theme

CLOSE READING **Tip of the Week**

When I **reread**, I notice how the author appeals to my five senses.

Russell

Write The imagery connects to the theme by conveying _____

_____

_____

? How does the poet use Pablo's shoes to convey the theme of this poem?

Talk About It Reread the poem on page 508. Talk with a partner about how the poet describes the tennis shoes.

Cite Text Evidence What words and phrases describe the tennis shoes? Write text evidence in the web and tell the poem's theme.

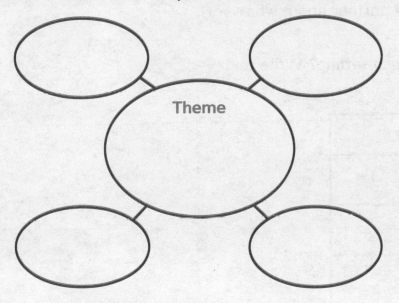

Theme

Write The poet uses Pablo's shoes to convey theme by _____

_____

_____

 QUICK TIP

I can use these sentence frames when I talk poetry.

This kind of poem is called a . . .

This style of poetry is characterized by . . .

Your Turn

Compare how each poet shares his common message of the importance of taking a break. Cite evidence from the text using these sentence frames to organize your text evidence.

Each poet uses imagery to . . .

This helps me visualize . . .

Go Digital!
Write your response online.

"Drumbeat"
"Sittin' on the Dock of the Bay"

? How does the author help you visualize the setting in the poem "Drumbeat"?

Talk About It Reread the poem on page 510. Talk with a partner about what each stanza describes.

Cite Text Evidence What words and phrases describe each setting? Write text evidence in the chart.

City	Country

Write The author helps me visualize setting by _____

_____

_____

? **How does the language of these poems show the poets' points of view?**

COLLABORATE

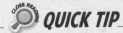
QUICK TIP
When I reread, I notice the point of view of the poet.

Talk About It Reread the two poems on pages 510 and 511. With a partner, determine the point of view of each poem.

Cite Text Evidence What phrases help you figure out the point of view? Write text evidence and explain.

Point of View	Text Evidence

Write The poet's words and phrases describe two distinct points of view that

say _____

_____

? How do the song writer and the poets who wrote "To You", "Sittin' on the Dock of the Bay", and "I Don't Care if the Rain Comes Down" share their points of view?

COLLABORATE

Talk About It Read the song lyrics. Talk with a partner about what the song means. Discuss why the writer uses repetition.

Cite Text Evidence Circle words and phrases that help you understand what the mood of the song is. Underline how the narrator feels about dancing.

Write I know how the song writer and the poets feel because

_____

_____

_____

_____

CLOSE READING
QUICK TIP
I can use words and phrases in the song to help me understand how the writer feels. This will help me compare it to text.

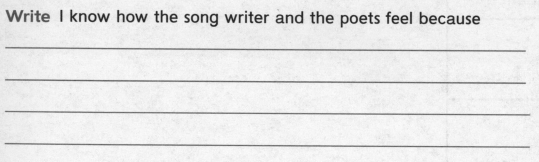

"I Don't Care if the Rain Comes Down"

American Folk Song

I don't care if the rain comes down,

I'm gonna dance all day,

I don't care if the rain comes down,

I'm gonna dance all day.

Hey, hey, carry me away,

I'm gonna dance all day,

Hey, hey, carry me away,

I'm gonna dance all day.

AlohaHawaii/Shutterstock